Hitler's
BERCHTESGADEN

A GUIDE TO THIRD REICH SITES
IN THE BERCHTESGADEN
AND OBERSALZBERG AREA

GEOFFREY R. WALDEN

FONTHILL

This book is dedicated to the memory of my father, Captain Delbert R. Walden,
U.S. Army Air Corps, whose visits to Berchtesgaden in 1945 and 1946
inspired my writing.

Fonthill Media Limited
Fonthill Media LLC
www.fonthillmedia.com
office@fonthillmedia.com

First published in the United Kingdom and the United States of America 2014

ISBN 978-1-78155-226-1

Typeset in Mrs Eaves XL Serif Narrow 10.5pt on 13.5pt

Contents

Artist Ludwig Hohlwein depicted Berchtesgaden. See page 52

Preface

This book grew out of research to discover the locations of photographs taken by my father, an ordnance officer in the U.S. Army Air Corps stationed in Germany as part of the Army of Occupation from 1945 to 1946. When I followed my father's footsteps in 1979, as a U.S. Army lieutenant stationed in Germany during the Cold War, I travelled around Bavaria to find the sites my father had visited and photographed some thirty-five years previously. I had learned that my father was stationed outside Munich, but his photographs made it clear that he spent a great deal of time in the Berchtesgaden area, staying in the Berchtesgadener Hof hotel and relaxing at the Königssee lake with his German *Fräulein*, and also visiting the Eagle's Nest and the ruins of the Third Reich buildings on the Obersalzberg.

I first visited Berchtesgaden and the Obersalzberg during a trip to the Armed Forces Recreation Center in the summer of 1981. Using Josef Geiss' book *Obersalzberg* and the *After the Battle* magazine issue on the Obersalzberg as guides, I spent an exciting week visiting the General Walker Hotel and other Third Reich-era buildings and exploring the ruins and tunnels on the Obersalzberg.

Since that first visit I have been stationed in Germany with the U.S. Army for three more tours totaling twelve years, and I have spent many weeks on the Obersalzberg. Eventually I began to give tours to visiting friends, since many of the Third Reich sites are not listed in tour books, and the ruins sites in the woods can be difficult to find. I was fortunate to meet a fellow explorer named Ralf Hornberger, who has become a life-long friend and who first showed me several of the sites in this book. We have spent many pleasant hours researching historical records, photos, and maps, and exploring the Obersalzberg together.

Acknowledgements

Ralf and Tatjana Hornberger have welcomed me into their home and spent many hours with me in Berchtesgaden and on the 'Berg. Ralf reviewed the manuscript of this book and made many valuable suggestions. The late Frau Ingrid Scharfenberg, owner of the Hotel zum Türken on the Obersalzberg, became a dear friend of mine during my numerous stays at her historic hotel, and she told me many wonderful stories about the area's history during hours of conversation. Noted local historian Florian Beierl, Jeff Carson, and Jacqueline Wilson provided much valuable information. My family and I enjoyed the company of our friends Ed and P. J. Matthews, Randall Lee Rose and Julie Chaney, and Ray and Gilda Northcott on repeat visits to the Obersalzberg. Frank Huber, administrator of the Hinterbrand Lodge (former Dietrich Eckart Hütte), was kind enough to give me a tour inside this historic building. In spite of all the help and information I have received from all of these wonderful people, any errors in this book are solely my own responsibility.

Two major sources were used for photos, both in the U.S. National Archives, Still Pictures Branch, Archives II, College Park, Maryland: Record Group 242, Heinrich Hoffmann Photo Collection and Eva Braun Photo Albums, and Record Group 111SC, U.S. Army Signal Corps Collection. Marc Romanych of the Digital History Archive and Dr. Hans-Georg Carls of the Luftbild Datenbank provided copies of some photos from the National Archives. I am grateful to Nancy Tarsitano Drake and David Dionne for supplying several photos from their collections.

The staffs of the following museums and collections were more than helpful during my research visits: 101st Airborne Division Museum, Fort Campbell, Kentucky; Fort Stewart Museum, Fort Stewart, Georgia; U.S. Army Infantry Museum, Fort Benning, Georgia; U.S. Army Military History Institute, Carlisle Barracks, Pennsylvania; U.S. Army Armor School Library, Fort Knox, Kentucky; Imperial War Museum, London, England.

Last but very far from least, I owe a huge debt of gratitude to my wife Deborah and daughter Erin, who cheerfully accompanied me on many trips of exploration and relaxation in Berchtesgaden – their company made it all so much more enjoyable!

Ansbach, Germany
June 2013

Introduction
Why This Book?

The Berchtesgaden area was changed forever when Adolf Hitler moved there in 1925. Hitler and other Nazi leaders had luxurious homes on the Obersalzberg, a mountain area overlooking Berchtesgaden, and a large compound of barracks, administration, and housing was constructed there. Hitler entertained world leaders in his Berghof home, where decisions were made that changed the course of history. Indeed, the Berchtesgaden–Obersalzberg area was one of Hitler's 'Führer Headquarters' during the Second World War. The Obersalzberg was bombed by the Royal Air Force in April 1945, reducing many of the buildings to ruins. The U.S. Army occupied this ruined area in May 1945 and continued to administer it until 1952. As a condition to returning the area to nominal German control, the ruins of Hitler's Berghof and other prominent buildings were razed.

Where did 'Nazi' come from?
The popular interpretation of the origin of the name 'Nazi' is a contraction of the German pronunciation of *Nationalsozialismus*, or National Socialism (the Nazi Party's official name in English was the National Socialist German Workers Party – NSDAP). However, 'Nazi' was more likely adopted from a Bavarian/Austrian nickname for a fool, and was initially applied by opponents of Hitler's politics. Socialists were popularly called 'Sozis', so the National Socialists became 'Nazis'. However, Hitler and the members of his party disliked this name, instead calling themselves 'National Socialists' or *Parteigenossen* – Party comrades.

However, the American forces retained control of several hotels and buildings in the area to use as a recreation center for soldiers and their families. From the mid-1950s until 1995, the Berchtesgaden Recreation Center was a showpiece for the American military. With the drawdown of U.S. forces in Germany following the end of the Cold War, the Berchtesgaden portion of the American Forces Recreation Center was finally returned to complete German control.

During the period when the American Forces Recreation Center operated the General Walker Hotel (former Platterhof), the Skyline Lodge and golf course (former Gutshof complex), and the Evergreen Lodge (Albert Speer's former architectural studio), little was done with the ruins in the area. Even though the area had been officially returned to German control in 1952, in actual practice the U.S. Army exercised *de facto* control over most of the Third Reich buildings and ruins remaining on the Obersalzberg. The Berghof site was partially buried and planted with trees, but the garage remained intact. The basements of the SS barracks buildings remained beneath a soccer field, and other nearby ruins such as the greenhouse, Guest House, Kindergarten, and Platterhof garage also remained.

With the return of the entire Obersalzberg area to the Bavarian government in 1995, these embarrassing remains posed a problem. The authorities did not wish to refurbish or preserve any of these buildings, and they embarked on a program of further razing of the Third Reich buildings and ruins, demonstrating the extreme difficulty that Germany still often experiences in dealing with its Nazi past. The ruined garage of Hitler's Berghof house was demolished in late 1995, immediately following the U.S. Army's return of control of the area. The Bavarian government leased the Obersalzberg to the Gewerbegrund company (a wholly-owned subsidiary of the Bavarian State Bank), and from 1999 to 2004 Gewerbegrund demolished the Platterhof hotel and its garage, tore down most of the Guest House ruin and built a museum on its foundation, and removed the Kindergarten ruins and the adjacent basements of the SS Kaserne buildings. Concurrently, much of the high hill that dominated the Obersalzberg, sometimes called Göring's Hill, was bulldozed away and a modern InterContinental Resort Hotel was built on what was left of the hill, obliterating the site of Göring's house and removing other ruins associated with the underground tunnel systems.

Just as the 1952 destruction of Hitler's ruined Berghof was hotly debated in the local press, these later projects of destruction and construction on the Obersalzberg have not proceeded without controversy. Those interested in history have criticised the destruction of the remaining buildings, particularly the former Platterhof hotel, parts of which dated back hundreds of years. Some visiting historians expressed dismay while the Third Reich ruins were being removed in 2001–2002, without any attempt at historical study or preservation, and the Bavarian Monument Protection office went on record in 2009 as saying that the Obersalzberg buildings and ruins, including the site of Hitler's Berghof, should be on the list of protected historic sites, and the ruins had been demolished without clearance. The destruction continued when the famous Berchtesgadener Hof hotel was torn down, the ruins of Hitler's Tea House were removed, and the housing wing of the Gutshof was demolished in 2006 to 2007. No matter how many historic buildings and ruins are removed, the history of what happened on the Obersalzberg during the Third Reich cannot be erased or hidden.

The InterContinental Hotel found itself in the center of controversy when it opened in March 2005. Many local residents would have preferred to see the area returned to a quiet vacation destination, as it was prior to 1933, without a large glass and steel hotel overlooking the entire area, with its associated traffic and noise. Due to its location overlooking the site of Adolf Hitler's house and adjacent to the site of Hermann Göring's house (not to mention Martin Bormann's tunnel system in the mountain directly beneath), the hotel was quickly dubbed the 'Hotel Hitler' by the media. The Simon Wiesenthal Center and others criticised the hotel as an attempt to bring fun and relaxation to a location that is so closely associated with the Nazi dictator. Despite the Bavarian government's attempt to turn the Obersalzberg into a high-scale resort area by building and operating the InterContinental hotel there, a leading Munich newspaper revealed in 2010 that the

InterContinental had lost some fifteen million euros (about twenty million dollars) since it was opened in 2005.

Keeping the controversy alive, some sensational statements in various print and television media have claimed that the ruin sites have become a mecca for 'Braun' tourists – neo-Nazis and 'Hitler pilgrims' – and thus all traces of the Third Reich should be erased from the area. Indeed, Bavarian government officials have stated their apprehension over the Obersalzberg becoming a neo-Nazi gathering site as a reason to remove the remaining Third Reich buildings and ruins. Perhaps a surer method to deter any such 'Nazi tourism' would be to open the entire area as a historic site, complete with historically accurate interpretive markers at the relevant locations, similar to what the city of Nuremberg has done with its considerable remains of the Third Reich.

These claims about neo-Nazis and 'Hitler pilgrims' on the Obersalzberg are frankly divorced from reality! There has never been a neo-Nazi rally on the Obersalzberg. Although votive candles and Nazi-related graffiti have appeared at some of the sites, this phenomenon has mostly disappeared since the sites have become more regularly visited by an interested public. I have visited the Obersalzberg many times since 1981, in almost every month of the year. I have stayed in local hotels and guesthouses and interviewed local residents. I have also spoken with visitors from the United States, Great Britain, Canada, Spain, Belgium, the Netherlands, Germany, other European countries, and as far away as Australia, New Zealand, and Japan. None of these people were neo-Nazis or wished to glorify Hitler – all had a sincere interest in the history of the period, including the role of the Obersalzberg in that history.

Naturally, due to the immense importance of the Second World War in our history, Hitler and the Nazis continue to fascinate people, and exploring historic sites and ruins is a pleasurable hobby for many. From my perspective, the great majority of those who visit the area today do not do so out of any admiration for Hitler and his policies, but rather to experience for themselves where these historic events happened, and to contemplate firsthand the sites associated with a regime that caused the deaths of millions of people and wrought such change on the world with such long-lasting effects.

This guide book is written to help such history-minded explorers. Most mainstream tourism books, if they mention the Obersalzberg at all, describe the Eagle's Nest, often confusing this with Hitler's Berghof house. Even some guide books from well-known publishing houses state that there is nothing left to see of the Nazi past on the Obersalzberg except the Eagle's Nest; others claim that the Eagle's Nest was demolished at the end of the Second World War.

When journalist Paul Moor visited Berchtesgaden in 1951 he found no directions to the Obersalzberg ruins: 'the question seemed to have become a hot potato, something that someone, apparently, by pretending it wasn't there, was hoping would go away'. Ironically, very little has changed in the intervening sixty years. The authorities still, apparently, pretend that the remains of the Nazi past are not there. The history buff who actually travels to the Obersalzberg and inquires about the Third Reich past is given very little help from staff at local displays and museums. This guide book will lead you to many of the sites that can still be found, both on the Obersalzberg and in Berchtesgaden and the surrounding area.

In describing a shade tree that was planted at the Berghof, Hitler's photographer Heinrich Hoffmann wrote in 1955 that 'everything which had the slightest connection with the previous owner of the Berghof was blown to pieces, and a little later it was all razed to the ground once again. All that now remains is this tree, and I can only hope that what I have just now described will not cause it, too, to disappear'. Hoffmann's premonition came true, and Hitler's shade tree was cut down in the 1960s. To close this introduction I can only echo Hoffmann's sentiment, in the hope that describing these sites in this book will not lead to their further destruction.

Hints for Visitors

Please be aware of the following notes and cautions while touring the area:

The sites and directions in this book were current as of publication, but due to ongoing construction projects on the Obersalzberg and in the Berchtesgaden area, visitors may find that some roads, trails, and parking areas have changed. I recommend you visit the Berchtesgaden Tourism Office (*Kurdirektion* – across from the train station) and get a current map of the area.

Automobile odometer readings are approximate, and are meant as a guide to prepare you for upcoming turns, not as an exact indication of distances. The GPS information is similarly given as approximate location guides, since GPS devices can differ from each other. Times shown for each tour are approximate normal times spent by most visitors.

Be aware that Berchtesgaden is a mountain town, and streets and roads in the area can be quite narrow. Parking is often at a premium in Berchtesgaden itself. Use caution on the roads leading to the Obersalzberg – these are narrow, curving mountain roads, with some of the steepest grades in Germany. Use extra caution going downhill here – it is easy to overheat your automobile brakes if you are not prepared for this.

If you do not have your own transportation, you can still take the walking tours in this book and visit some of the other sites. Bus service runs regularly from the train station in Berchtesgaden up to the Obersalzberg bus stop for the Dokumentation Obersalzberg display and the Eagle's Nest (Kehlsteinhaus) bus ticket office. You can also use the bus to reach the Königssee, Ramsau/Hintersee, Rossfeld, and other area destinations. Local bus schedules are available at the train station or the Tourist Information Office (*Kurdirektion*) across the river. Bus transportation is free using your *Kurkarte* (hotel guest card).

Finally, nothing in this guide book should be construed as advice to trespass on private property.

CHAPTER 1

Berchtesgaden and the Obersalzberg in the Third Reich

In 1925, Adolf Hitler chose a remote mountain resort area in the southeast corner of Bavaria as his home. Berchtesgaden was a small town that catered (then as now) to the tourist trade – folks who enjoyed a winter or summer in the Alps, as well as those who sought a cure for respiratory ailments in the clear mountain air. Hitler had visited the area previously in 1923 to confer with his mentor Dietrich Eckart, and following his release from prison after the abortive Munich putsch attempt of November 1923, Hitler returned to Berchtesgaden to finish his book *Mein Kampf*. Eventually he settled in a small house on the Obersalzberg, an isolated locale in the mountains overlooking Berchtesgaden, making the area his *Wahlheimat* – his chosen home. From Hitler's house he could look past the Untersberg mountain to Salzburg in his native Austria, in the distance.

After Hitler became Chancellor of Germany in 1933, the Obersalzberg was transformed into the southern seat of power for the Nazi Party. Largely orchestrated by Party leader Martin Bormann, many local farmers and landowners were forced to sell their properties and move away, and the buildings were torn down. All of this was to make way for a massive building project that consumed Bormann's attention until the end of the Second World War. Eventually, the Obersalzberg was closed to the general public, because here Hitler had his lavish Berghof home, and here were located houses for Luftwaffe chief Hermann Göring, architect Albert Speer, and Bormann himself. This seat of power required barracks for the SS guard force and the small army of construction workers, houses and buildings for the administration of the area, a model farm and greenhouse for Bormann's agricultural pursuits, a large hotel, associated adjutants' quarters, and Hitler's famed Eagle's Nest. Other Nazi buildings were erected in Berchtesgaden and the surrounding villages. Eventually, the mountain itself was honeycombed with some four miles of tunnels and air raid shelters. Until it was bombed by the Royal Air Force on 25 April 1945, construction work did not stop on the Obersalzberg.

When Hitler moved in, Haus Wachenfeld was a simple wooden mountain chalet.

Why Do We Say *THE* Obersalzberg?

Germans have always considered 'Obersalzberg' to be the name of a region, not a town as such, so to speak of 'der Obersalzberg' is to describe the entire area. 'Obersalzberg' means 'over the salt mountain', and the Obersalzberg area is indeed located on the mountain above the famous salt mine in Berchtesgaden. Since the Germans refer to the area as 'der Obersalzberg', this books uses '*the* Obersalzberg'.

Contrary to some claims, the Obersalzberg buildings were not built by 'slave labor' or concentration camp prisoners. Some of the skilled stonework artisans and general construction laborers came from outside Germany, and the hours were long with sometimes arduous working conditions (particularly building the Kehlsteinhaus and road and the air raid shelters), but the workers were paid for their labor and allowed vacations to return to their homes.

The Obersalzberg area, and particularly Hitler's Berghof house, are often called Hitler's 'retreat', but this is a misnomer. Although Hitler had an apartment in Munich, and he spent much time in the chancellor's residence in Berlin and in his field headquarters during the Second World War, the Berghof was always his primary home, not a vacation house. In his recorded wartime 'table talks' (published in 1953 as *Hitler's Secret Conversations*), Hitler said, 'I had become immediately attached to the Obersalzberg. I'd fallen in love with the landscape.' He described the Berghof as a 'truly ideal situation' because it faced Salzburg, 'perhaps out of

Hitler had his original house rebuilt into the Berghof, a showpiece to impress visitors.

a nostalgia for my little fatherland'. 'Yes, there are so many links between the Obersalzberg and me. So many things were born there, and brought to fruition there. I've spent up there the finest hours of my life.'

Albert Speer, Hitler's architect and confidant, recorded that Hitler used the peace of the Obersalzberg to write his most important speeches there. Hitler's adjutant Wilhelm Brückner wrote that important conversations occurred on the Obersalzberg before great decisions were made. Hitler himself reminisced, 'My thoughts remain faithful to my first house. It's there that all my great projects were conceived and ripened.'

Hitler first made a permanent residence on the Obersalzberg when he rented a small mountain chalet called 'Haus Wachenfeld' in 1927 or 1928, which he purchased in 1933. The initial house had only some eight rooms and no garage or driveway. A series of remodelings in 1933 and 1934 added a garage and drive, along with a sunroom, terrace, and other improvements. In 1936 the house was rebuilt into the palatial Berghof, retaining parts of the old house, but adding some forty rooms, including a great hall measuring 27 by 13 meters (89 by 43 feet). A huge picture window with 90 separate panes of glass, measuring 9 by 3.6 meters (29.5 by 11.8 feet), allowed a grand view of the mountains to the north and could be lowered into its casing for an open-air experience. Hitler had a large study next to his bedroom, which shared a bath with the adjacent bedroom of his mistress Eva Braun. A pine-paneled dining room with an attached breakfast nook seated twenty-four. The basement housed heating and storage rooms and even a small bowling alley. Interior decorations included marble fireplaces, tile ovens, and valuable paintings and tapestries, one of which could be moved to show films on the wall behind. Further additions were made to the house in 1938.

The Berghof perched on the side of the mountains overlooking Berchtesgaden.

Hitler's Berghof is sometimes erroneously called the 'Eagle's Nest', and this name is also sometimes applied to the entire Obersalzberg complex. This misnomer seems to have originated with U.S. Army soldiers or American journalists in 1945, some of whom were apparently confused about Hitler's house, or mistakenly thought that it was called 'Eagle's Nest'. However, this name is properly applied only to the building on the Kehlstein mountain above the Obersalzberg – the Kehlsteinhaus (see Chapter 4).

MAJOR THIRD REICH CONSTRUCTION SITES IN THE BERCHTESGADEN AREA

Adolf Hitler Youth Hostel
Strub

Airfield buildings, Ainring
Used by Adolf Hitler and other Nazi leaders to fly to the Berchtesgaden area

Air raid shelter tunnel systems
Six tunnel systems constructed in the hills beneath Berchtesgaden, and additional tunnels

were built in the Wemholz area, Hotel Geiger, and the Mountain Troops Barracks (none of these are open to the public today).

Anti-aircraft flak battery positions
Some fourteen batteries of heavy and light flak guns were emplaced around the Berchtesgaden area from 1943 to 1945.

Bahnhof – train station with post office

Barracks complex – for Mountain Troops, Strub

Berchtesgadener Hof hotel
(conversion of an existing building)

Camp Vockenbichl
SS Barracks, Oberau

Chancellery complex (Kanzlei)
Stanggass

Dietrich Eckart Hospital
Stanggass

Hermann Göring's hunting lodge
Roth (Königssee area)

Hitler Youth Home
Oberau

Luftwaffe building complex – Am Wemholz

Schießstättbrücke guard house

Sport School – for the League of German Girls (BDM), Strub

Train tunnel – to Salzburg

MAJOR THIRD REICH CONSTRUCTION SITES ON THE OBERSALZBERG

Air raid shelter tunnel systems
Over 6.4 km (four miles) of tunnel systems (*Stollen*) at various levels were built into the mountains to provide protection against bombing attacks for the Obersalzberg inhabitants and workers. Not all of these tunnel systems were completed by 25 April 1945, but they still provided shelter for thousands during the attack. The following tunnel systems were built or started:

– Antenberg Stollen, for construction workers at the Antenberg camp
– Berghof Stollen, for Adolf Hitler and Eva Braun, and closest staff
– Bormann Stollen, for Martin Bormann and his family
– Buchenhöhe Stollen, for inhabitants of the Buchenhöhe housing complex
– Göring Stollen, for Hermann Göring and his family and staff
– Hintereck Stollen, for inhabitants of the Hintereck and Klaushöhe housing areas
– Platterhof/Gästehaus Stollen, for staff of the Platterhof hotel, Nazi Party offices staff, and military hospital staff and patients
– SS Munitions Stollen, built to store explosives and munitions
– SS Stollen, for the SS guard and work force at the SS Barracks
– Verbindungs Stollen, various tunnels connecting these systems and other buildings; the largest of these was the tunnel running between Bormann's tunnel, past the Hotel zum Türken, to Hitler's tunnel.
– Vordereck Stollen, command and control center for the air raid warning system and anti-aircraft batteries, also for the Kindergarten and administration building personnel
– A further 'deep system' was begun at a level some 100 meters lower than the central Obersalzberg tunnel systems. This system of huge tunnels would have provided underground vehicular access into the interior of the Obersalzberg, and may have been planned as protection from atomic weapons. Excavations were made near the Gutshof farm and in the Obertal area, extending toward the center of the Obersalzberg, and a shaft was begun in Hitler's shelter to reach this lower level, but these projects were never completed.

Albert Speer's architectural studio

Barracks camps for construction workers
Over a dozen camps with wooden barracks buildings were established in the area, the largest of these being at the Antenberg, Dürreck, Ligeretalm, Obertal, Riemerfeld, Scharitzkehlalm, and Winkl (north of Berchtesgaden).

Berghof
Adolf Hitler's house, converted from the earlier 'Haus Wachenfeld' chalet

Buchenhöhe housing area

Eagle's Nest (Kehlsteinhaus) – with access road and tunnel

Gutshof farm complex
(including a greenhouse, two bee houses, dairy buildings, pig sty, hay barn)

Hermann Göring's house and Adjutancy

Hintereck housing area with coal bunker

Hotel zum Türken
(conversion of an earlier building)

Kindergarten complex

Klaushöhe housing area

Martin Bormann's house (conversion of an earlier building)

Platterhof hotel complex
with guesthouse and employee housing/garage (partial conversion from earlier buildings)

SS Barracks complex
including administration buildings, garage, underground rifle range

Tea House

Theater Hall

Youth Boarding Home

The Obersalzberg was not a bombing target until 1945, when it was bombed to prevent Hitler or Nazi forces from retreating there to carry on a last-ditch defense of the Reich. Accordingly, 375 heavy bombers of the Royal Air Force attacked the Obersalzberg compound in two waves on 25 April 1945, dropping over 1,200 tons of bombs. This British bombing attack in the final days of the Second World War in Europe turned Hitler's Berghof, the SS barracks, Bormann's and Göring's houses, and several other buildings into ruins. The local population plundered these ruins during the next week, taking many valuable resources such as food and building materials. In mid-afternoon of 4 May 1945, retreating SS soldiers set fire to Hitler's ruined Berghof, doing as much or more damage to the structure than the bombing. Allied forces reached Berchtesgaden and the Obersalzberg shortly thereafter and found the Berghof still on fire.

On the afternoon of 4 May 1945, soldiers of the 3rd U.S. Infantry Division captured the still-smoking Berghof ruin.

Exactly *which* Allied forces reached the area first and captured the Nazi seat of power on the Obersalzberg has been debated ever since. In 1945 it was generally acknowledged that American soldiers from the 3rd Infantry Division were the first to reach and occupy Berchtesgaden and the Obersalzberg. It was not until the 1992 publication of Stephen Ambrose's history of a company of the 101st Airborne Division, *Band of Brothers*, and especially after the 2001 television mini-series based on the book, that serious debate occurred. Ambrose's book and the mini-series claimed that E Company, 506th Parachute Infantry Regiment of the U.S. 101st Airborne Division were the first Allied soldiers to reach Berchtesgaden, the Obersalzberg, and even the Eagle's Nest. In reality, these soldiers did not reach Berchtesgaden until 5 May 1945, the day following the arrival of other American and French soldiers.

So, who *did* capture Berchtesgaden and the Obersalzberg? In early May 1945 'everybody and his brother' wanted to get to Berchtesgaden first, and in the years since it has sometimes seemed that everyone wanted to claim credit. Although Berchtesgaden was not in the sector assigned to the U.S. 3rd Infantry Division, Major General John 'Iron Mike' O'Daniel was determined that his division should claim the prize, and he had received orders from U.S. 7th Army commander General Alexander Patch to take Berchtesgaden. Since he controlled the only useable bridge in the area, O'Daniel delayed other troops until he received word that battalions from his 7th Infantry Regiment had reached the town shortly before 4:00 o'clock on the afternoon of 4 May 1945. These 3rd Infantry Division soldiers cleared the town and then drove up the mountain to the Obersalzberg, where they hauled down the Nazi flag in front of Hitler's bombed and smoking Berghof home (the flag was torn into strips and distributed as souvenirs among the 3rd Infantry Division soldiers). The mayor of Berchtesgaden formally surrendered the town to Lieutenant-Colonel Kenneth Wallace of O'Daniel's 7th Infantry Regiment. Berchtesgaden and the Obersalzberg had been captured and occupied by the U.S. 3rd Infantry Division.

These soldiers hauled down the Nazi flag from in front of Hitler's house.

During the night of 4–5 May, having been delayed by Major General O'Daniel's bridge-guarding, the French 2nd Armored Division arrived in Berchtesgaden and was assigned to the Obersalzberg, which was being guarded by soldiers of the 3rd Infantry Division. These Frenchmen were likely the first to reach the Eagle's Nest high above the Obersalzberg, since the mountain road and the entrance to the elevator tunnel were blocked by heavy snow which would have likely deterred any adventurous American explorers that night. The lead elements of the U.S. 101st Airborne Division also began to arrive that night, with the 506th Parachute Infantry Regiment arriving the next morning around 10:00 a.m.

Other individuals, including communications soldiers from the U.S. 3rd Infantry Division and an officer from the French 2nd Armored Division, claimed to have driven jeeps up to the Obersalzberg before the U.S. 7th Infantry Regiment soldiers arrived and captured the ruins, but these accounts describe the Berghof as completely intact with no bomb damage, or not set on fire until late on the afternoon of 4 May, neither of which was the case. Whenever they arrived, these jeep-mounted troops spent only a short time on the Obersalzberg, because they did not have the military strength to seize and occupy the area. This was left to organised units of the U.S. 3rd Infantry Division, until they were relieved during the night of 4–5 May 1945 by the French 2nd Armored Division, who were in turn relieved by the U.S. 101st Airborne Division on 6 May. But the units that arrived first and captured Berchtesgaden and the Obersalzberg belonged to the U.S. 3rd Infantry Division, the famous 'Rock of the Marne'.

At first, confusion reigned in Berchtesgaden and on the Obersalzberg. Elated at taking the last Nazi stronghold, and having liberated large stocks of hoarded wine and liquor, many

Allied soldiers were provided with a map showing the locations of the major Obersalzberg buildings, but inaccuracies indicate this map was made before May 1945.

Hitler's driveway led past the ruins of the Berghof on the right, with the Hotel zum Türken behind it, and Martin Bormann's bombed house on the hill in the distance.

Allied soldiers went on a spree of drinking, plundering and destruction. The French soldiers in particular were reported to be 'out of control' by the U.S. 3rd Infantry Division Operations Officer, as they shot up a trainload of Hermann Göring's valuable artworks and gangs roamed through the town, apparently seeking revenge for the German occupation of France. The French Moroccan soldiers are remembered by local residents for numerous rapes in the area, and drunken soldiers murdered German civilians. The 3rd Infantry Division had returned to its assigned area near Salzburg, but order was slowly restored after the 101st Airborne Division took over control of Berchtesgaden and the Obersalzberg on 6 May 1945.

The U.S. Army occupied the Berchtesgaden area in May 1945, and because of its associations with Hitler and the Nazis, the Americans continued to administer the Obersalzberg until 1952. When the military occupation authorities turned over administration to the local government, the U.S. Army retained three Obersalzberg buildings as hotels for a military recreation area, but most of the Third Reich buildings and ruins were razed, for fear they would become shrines for die-hard ex-Nazis. The ruins of Hitler's Berghof were dynamited on 30 April 1952, the seventh anniversary of his death in Berlin. However, the Eagle's Nest was spared because of its tourism potential.

Even after the Allied military government ceased to officially administer the Obersalzberg, in actual practice, the U.S. Army remained in control and built a golf course and ski runs near its Obersalzberg hotels. The Berchtesgaden Recreation Area provided relaxation for hundreds of thousands of American service members and their families. American troops remained stationed at the former *Kanzlei* complex in the Berchtesgaden suburb of Stanggass, which was used by the Armed Forces Recreation Center as its headquarters. Following the drawdown of U.S. forces in Germany in the early 1990s, the American facilities in the Berchtesgaden area were closed and the Obersalzberg was returned to complete German control in late 1995.

Before being demolished in 1952, the ruins of Hitler's Berghof served as a set for the film *The Devil Makes Three*.

The Berghof ruins were demolished by explosives on 30 April 1952, the seventh anniversary of Hitler's death in Berlin.

CHAPTER 2

Berchtesgaden Area Tours

NOTE: Directions for all driving tours begin at the Bahnhof (train station – GPS N47.6262, E13.0000, Bahnhofsplatz 1). The Tourist Information Center (*Kurdirektion*) is directly opposite, across the river (you can modify these directions from other start points, such as various hotels). There is a large parking lot behind the train station, on the other side of the tracks, reached by an access street called Salinenplatz, a short distance down the street from the Bahnhof, toward the main part of town (GPS N47.6280, E13.0011). This is a pay parking lot that requires a *Parkschein* parking ticket, which is purchased from a small machine at the side of the lot (see the Hints for Parking in Appendix B).

DRIVING TOUR NO. 1

U.S. Army Occupation of Berchtesgaden, May 1945, Berchtesgaden Area Chancellery, Dietrich Eckart Hospital

This tour takes about one hour driving and viewing time. Leave Berchtesgaden toward the west (turn toward the right away from the train station) on highway B20/B305 and turn north (right) at 2.0 km (1.2 miles) onto highway B20 toward Bad Reichenhall. Just as you leave Bischofswiesen (going under the overpass), the mountain that you see straight in front of you is called the *Schlafende Hexe* – the Sleeping Witch. A little imagination can picture a witch sleeping on her back, head to the right, with a craggy nose and jutting chin, but with a youthful looking 'breast' just to the left. The Witch can be seen from many locations in the Berchtesgaden area, including the Kehlsteinhaus (Eagle's Nest) and the Königssee lake.

At 9.0 km (5.6 miles), pull into the bus stop area at the village of Winkl and park in the lot on the right side of the road (GPS N47.6653, E12.9512, Von Eichendorff Strasse). On 4 May 1945, District Commissioner Karl Theodor Jacob met the advancing American troops of the 3rd Infantry Division here, to surrender Berchtesgaden without a fight. Looking back down the road toward Berchtesgaden gives the same view as this photo from that occasion (the photographer's viewpoint was on the opposite side of the road, across from the parking area – exercise caution if you cross the road here).

A tunnel system was begun in early 1945 in the hills across the highway from Winkl, designed as an underground installation to house part of the military high command in the event that

Soldiers of the U.S. 3rd Infantry Division on the way to Berchtesgaden meet local representatives north of the town.

the final defense of Germany took place in the 'Alpine Fortress' (the tunnel entrances are buried now and inaccessible). Although the Allies feared the possibility of such an 'Alpine Fortress', and there were plans to actually build several tunnel systems and bunkers in the Bavarian and Austrian Alps, no such 'National Redoubt' was ever completed, and Hitler and the German high command remained in Berlin through the downfall of the Third Reich. The present village of Winkl was built on the site of the barracks for the workers constructing these tunnels.

Drive into Winkl and follow Adalbert Stifter Strasse toward the church. Turn right in front of the *Sparkasse* (bank) onto Anton Guenther Strasse, and park in the lot on the other side of the church. At the far end of the lot is a memorial remembering the Germans who had settled the Sudeten area of Czechoslovakia, many of whom were killed or forced into exile in 1945.

Retrace your route through Winkl to highway B20 (the main road you came on).

(Note for the hungry – several good restaurants are along the road between Winkl and Berchtesgaden, or you can drive just up the road to the Panorama Park Einkaufszentrum (shopping center), which has an Italian cafe and a bakery.)

Original stones from the Berghof garage were used to construct the Wegmacher Chapel.

Optional – Turn right out of Winkl and proceed 5.3 km (3.3 miles) north on highway B20 and pass a small chapel at a pull-over on the left – use caution on this steep and curving mountain road (GPS N47.7077, E12.9271). Don't attempt to turn left here (it's illegal) – proceed 750 meters (0.5 mile) to a pull-over on the right side (just past a sharp right curve), and use that pull-over to turn around and head back uphill then turn right into the parking area for the chapel.

The chapel is called the Wegmacher Kapelle and it would be unremarkable but for one fact: it was built from the red marble blocks left over when the garage of Hitler's Berghof house on the Obersalzberg was demolished in 1995. Turn around and go back toward Berchtesgaden on B20, checking your odometer when you pass Winkl (end of Optional Tour).

Turn left out of Winkl and go back toward Berchtesgaden on B20, checking your odometer as you leave Winkl.

At 3.4 km (2.1 miles), turn left off B20, following the sign to Stanggass (this is Berchtesgadener Strasse). At 4.5 km (2.8 miles) (total from Winkl), turn right onto Urbanweg, at the fish shape sign that says *Forellenzucht*. Drive to the end of this street (0.5 km / 0.3 mile) and park in the lot at the flagpole (GPS N47.6313, E12.9748, Urbanweg 26). (Follow the street as it curves to the left and comes out into an open area, then turn right and park in the lot at the flagpole.)

This building complex was the Berchtesgaden area *Reichskanzlei*, a subsidiary of the Berlin Reichs Chancellery that was built in 1936 for the seat of government when Hitler was in residence at the Berghof. The eagle over the main doorway once grasped a wreathed swastika in its talons. This area included houses for military leaders Wilhelm Keitel, Chief of the General Staff (the large house opposite the main Chancellery building) and Alfred Jodl, Chief of the Operations Staff (a smaller house near the main Chancellery building – Jodl's original house was razed in 2006 and the modern house you see was built on the site). This complex was occupied by the U.S. Army in 1945, and served as the headquarters for the American

Forces Recreation Centers until 1995. It has been remodeled for apartments (the buildings on the left as you drove in here off the main street were also part of this complex). A large tunnel system beneath and behind the main building served as an air raid shelter (not open to the public).

Retrace your route to the main road (Berchtesgadener Strasse) and turn right toward Berchtesgaden. In about 85 meters (280 feet), turn left onto Sonnleitstrasse. Follow this street for 0.4 km (0.3 mile), and park in the lot on the left (GPS N47.6311, E12.9842, Sonnleitstrasse 33). The large building on the hill above, labeled Kurklinik Stanggass (now closed), was built in 1942 as the Dietrich Eckart Hospital, named in honor of Adolf Hitler's mentor (see Berchtesgaden Walking Tour No. 2). It served during the final period of the Second World War as a military convalescent hospital. The clinic has been closed for several years and the building is not open to the public.

Retrace your route to the main road (Berchtesgadener Strasse), and turn left toward Berchtesgaden. Just on the right after you turn are five similar houses in a row, visible behind the trees – these were part of the Dietrich Eckart Siedlung, a housing area built during the Third Reich period and named for Hitler's mentor. You can get a somewhat better view of these houses by turning right on Dr. Elschner Strasse, then right on Franz Geiger Strasse – the Dietrich Eckart Siedlung houses are along this street. Turn around and proceed back to the main road (Berchtesgadener Strasse) and turn right.

At 0.7 km (0.4 mile) you will pass the Hotel Geiger on the left (Berchtesgadener Strasse 111). This 19th century hotel (based on a 15th century farmhouse) catered to visiting European royalty, artists, and writers. During the Second World War the complex was used by the Luftwaffe Command, and Luftwaffe General Karl Koller had his headquarters there during the final two weeks of the war. An air raid tunnel system was installed in the hill behind the hotel. In the years after 1945 the posh hotel accommodated such prominent guests as John F. Kennedy (fresh out of the Navy and travelling through Germany as a journalist), Canadian Prime Minister Pierre Trudeau, Prince Albert of Monaco, and Elvis Presley. The hotel has been closed for several years.

Continue just downhill to the large left-hand curve. When you can see the town sign for Berchtesgaden on the right, you are at the site of this photo from 4 May 1945, showing a tank of the U.S. 3rd Infantry Division moving toward the town. A marker commemorating this event was placed here by veterans of the 3rd Infantry Division in 2011. There is a small private drive here to park in momentarily if you wish to view the marker (GPS N47.6262, E12.9899, Hanielstrasse 13).

Just downhill on the right is the site of the famous Berchtesgadener Hof hotel. The hotel, which had a long and important history, was torn down in 2006 to make way for a mountain museum. The Berchtesgadener Hof was originally the Grand Hotel Auguste Victoria and was remodeled by the Nazis in 1936 to 1938. Visiting dignitaries such as the Duke and Duchess of Windsor, Prime Minister Neville Chamberlain, and former Prime Minister David Lloyd George stayed here, as well as high-ranking Nazis such as Josef Goebbels, Heinrich Himmler, and Joachim von Ribbentrop. Eva Braun stayed here before she lived at the Berghof, and Field Marshal Erwin Rommel stayed in the Berchtesgadener Hof while visiting Hitler at the Berghof in 1944. Hitler's sister Paula lived here incognito as Frau Wolf in 1945 (see Berchtesgaden Driving Tour No. 4). Field Marshal Albert Kesselring surrendered to the U.S. Army here in May 1945. The American Forces Recreation Center used the Berchtesgadener Hof as its showpiece

The *Kanzlei* complex in Stanggass served as the southern Nazi headquarters when Hitler was in residence at his Berghof home.

The U.S. Army took over the *Kanzlei* complex in May 1945 and occupied it for fifty years.

The Dietrich Eckart hospital was named for Hitler's mentor.

The Hotel Geiger served as a Luftwaffe headquarters at the end of the war.

Tanks attached to the U.S. 3rd Infantry Division rolled into Berchtesgaden on 4 May 1945.

The famous Berchtesgadener Hof hotel hosted visiting soldiers of the U.S. 101st Airborne Division after the war.

hotel until 1995. Some of the Third Reich period outbuildings remain behind the hotel site (not open to the public).

You can go partway around the traffic circle to drive into the town center, or to return to the Bahnhof (train station), take the first right out of the traffic circle and proceed down the hill behind the Berchtesgadener Hof site. At the bottom of the hill turn left onto B305/B20, toward Berchtesgaden and the Bahnhof.

Driving Tour No. 2

Mountain Troops Barracks, BDM Sport School, Air Defense Bunker, and Adolf Hitler Youth Hostel

This tour takes about one hour. Turn west (right) from the Bahnhof on highway B305/B20 and drive toward Bad Reichenhall. At 1.0 km (0.6 mile) turn right, following the signs to Stanggass/Strub, and then left immediately toward Strub (turn left before the railroad tracks). At 1.0 km further (0.6 mile) you can park in the lot on the left behind the Lion Monument (GPS N47.6241, E12.9747, Gebirgsjägerstrasse 26). These buildings are the Mountain Troops Barracks (Gebirgsjäger Kaserne), built from 1936 to 1938. The Lion Monument is dedicated to the German Mountain Troops of the Second World War. The Kaserne was used by the U.S. Army after the war, but again is home to German Mountain Troops (the post is not open to the public, and photography is restricted).

Continue down the street, and turn right onto Dachmoosweg street, just past the church on the right. Take the second street to the left at the sign for Blumen Cramer, and park in the lot at the end (GPS N47.6249, E12.9689, Zum Steiner 9). In front of you, behind the florist shop, is a concrete bunker built for protection against air attack. The bunker is private property – please do not try to enter it or climb on it. The Cramer Florist Shop sells souvenirs, and the proprietors speak English.

Return to the main street and turn right. Continue past the west end of the barracks area to the end of this street and turn right onto highway B20. In 0.3 km (0.2 mile), turn right at the bus stop onto Insulaweg street, and immediately right again, following the signs to Insula. Park at the end of the street, as you reach the Altenheim buildings (GPS N47.6257, E12.9671, Insulaweg 1). This complex was built in 1938 as a Sports School for the Bund Deutscher Mädel (BDM) – the League of German Girls, or Hitler Youth organization for girls ages 14–18. It is now a home for the elderly (not open to the general public).

Retrace your route back past the Mountain Troops Barracks, and turn right onto Struberberg Strasse, following the sign that says Jugendherberge. Park in the lot beside the buildings, and walk back down the drive and look to the right (GPS N47.6246, E12.9798, Struberberg 8). This was the Adolf Hitler Jugendherberge (youth hostel) main building, built from 1935 to 1938 to house visiting Hitler Youth groups. The other buildings were also part of this complex, which still serves as a youth hostel and youth activities center. The main building retained its appearance from the Third Reich period until 2011, when it underwent a rather drastic remodeling.

Turn right out of the youth hostel drive, and drive down the hill and turn right and then left onto B305/B20 to return to Berchtesgaden.

This barracks for mountain troops was considered one of the most attractive designs for Third Reich period military barracks.

Only one above-ground air raid shelter was built in Berchtesgaden.

Poster artist Ludwig Hohlwein, who had a studio in Berchtesgaden after the war, portrayed the Bund Deutscher Mädel (BDM) sports activities for a 1934 propaganda poster. Girls like the one seen here would have trained at the BDM sports school in the Strub district of Berchtesgaden.

A youth hostel bearing Adolf Hitler's name was a popular site for Hitler Youth groups.

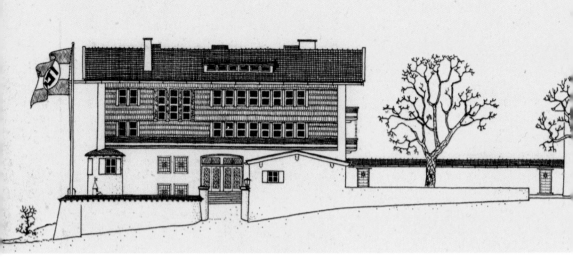

The youth hostel was remodeled in 2011, changing its 1936 appearance.

Driving Tour No. 3

Railroad Tunnel, SS Guard House, Nazi Rally Site

This tour takes about forty-five minutes. Start at the large parking lot behind the Bahnhof on Salinenplatz street (this is a pay lot during some periods of the day – you can buy a parking ticket at the *Parkschein* machine – see the Hints for Parking in Appendix B), and walk toward the large tunnel opening on the right of the parking lot entrance (GPS N47.6289, E13.0025). This tunnel was the beginning of a planned rail line to Salzburg, which was never completed. When Adolf Hitler took the train to Berchtesgaden, his special train was generally kept in this tunnel until his departure. In April 1945 one of Hermann Göring's luxury trains was parked in this tunnel, with a large collection of his personal belongings and artwork (the tunnel is not open to the public). The construction date of 1940 can still be seen on the upper right side of the tunnel opening, visible from the narrow street beside the Hotel Bavaria (Sunklergäßchen).

Walk into the lot toward the back of the Bahnhof, but keep to the right side, toward the hillside. On either end of the industrial building (Schnurrer Mineralöl) against the hill, you can see entrances to a tunnel system built into this hill for the protection of railway workers and others during air attack (this tunnel system is not open to the public). Six such tunnel systems, some with multiple levels, were built beneath the hills throughout Berchtesgaden to provide shelter for some 8,000–10,000 people. A little further from the building, back toward the train tunnel, is a small entrance to another tunnel, closed by a metal bunker door.

Return to your vehicle and leave the Bahnhof parking lot, turning left – stay to the right – do not drive uphill into town on Bahnhofstrasse. At the second traffic light turn right and immediately turn right into the small parking lot by the river (GPS N47.6303, E13.0061). Park here (this is also a pay lot requiring you to buy a *Parkschein* at the machine) and walk across the

Although this tunnel was built in 1940, the rail line was never completed.

Rail yard workers found shelter in this tunnel behind the rail station during the 1945 bombing attacks.

Visitors to the Obersalzberg had first to pass an SS guard house in Berchtesgaden.

The guard house at the Schießstätt Bridge was built in 1937.

SS personnel assigned to the Obersalzberg were issued passes for the various checkpoints.

road (carefully – watch for traffic coming both ways on this busy road) to the small building directly opposite with a sign that says Geschenk Lad'l (Bergwerkstrasse 101). This was the Schießstättbrücke guard house, marking the beginning of the exterior security zone for the Obersalzberg Nazi complex. The carved date 1937 can still be seen above the doorway. SS guards stationed here controlled access to the road leading uphill to the Obersalzberg.

Leave the parking lot at the opposite end and turn right. In 0.5 km (0.3 mile), just before the traffic light, turn left onto Koch Sternfeld Strasse. As you drive along Koch Sternfeld Strasse, on the left (just beyond the Penny Markt) is an open field where Adolf Hitler held a large Nazi rally in July 1932 (GPS N47.6359, E13.0077).

Continue on Koch Sternfeld Strasse and turn right onto Salzburger Strasse, then left onto highway B305 (toward Marktschellenberg and Salzburg). In 0.3 km (0.2 mile) turn right onto Bergwerkstrasse and cross the river. Along the street that goes up the hill behind the Gasthof Salzberg (Mieslötzweg street) are five similar houses along the right side. These were built at Hitler's order as housing for farmers and craftsmen who had been displaced by the sale of their property on the Obersalzberg.

Continuing on Bergwerkstrasse, you will pass the famous *Salzbergwerk* or Salt Mine. This is one of the main tourist attractions in Berchtesgaden – see Appendix A for further information. Further down Bergwerkstrasse is a sports field on the right. The *Sportplatz* was built in the 1930s, and the grandstand building is the original. Continue on Bergwerkstrasse, crossing the bridge, and turn left at the traffic light onto B305 to return to the Bahnhof.

Adolf Hitler reviewed a formation of SA men in Berchtesgaden in 1932.

Mountain Cemetery and Luftwaffe Recreation Center

This tour takes about ninety minutes. Take the traffic circle in front of the Bahnhof and turn right onto the road toward Schönau a.K. (not the nearby road toward Königssee). In 160 meters (520 feet) turn left following the sign to the *Bergfriedhof*. Park in the lot outside the *Bergfriedhof* cemetery and enter beside the chapel (GPS N47.6222, E12.9972, Am Friedhof 11). Follow the directions below to visit graves and cenotaphs of Second World War interest. At the far end of the cemetery is the *Helden Friedhof* – the Heroes Cemetery for war graves.

Colonel James B. Kraft – Walk around the right side of the chapel and through the cemetery gate – note that the gate handles are exactly the same style as the door handles in many of the Obersalzberg buildings, including Hitler's Berghof. Turn right at the first intersection, and walk along the hedge on the right. In the section on the left, just past the second path to the left, is the grave of American Colonel James Barry Kraft, first commander of the U.S. Army Berchtesgaden Recreation Area. He came to love Berchtesgaden so much that he wanted to be buried there.

Paula Hitler – Continue along the hedge on the right. Paula Hitler's grave is located in the first section on the right, past the end of the hedge (second row back, fifth grave plot). Paula was Adolf Hitler's only sibling who lived to adulthood. She lived most of the Third Reich period in relative obscurity in Vienna, but Hitler had her moved to Berchtesgaden to escape the Soviets advancing into Austria. After the war Paula continued to live a quiet life in Berchtesgaden until her death in 1960.

Paula Hitler's grave was marked until 2007, but although she is still buried in the plot, her name has been covered by a wooden plaque bearing the names of the Reif family, who owned the plot and were buried there in 2005–2006.

Ernst Maisel – Continue past Paula Hitler's grave to just past the first path on the left. On the left is a large marker for the grave of General Ernst Maisel, an infantry and staff officer in the Wehrmacht during the Second World War. He was one of the two generals who, on Hitler's orders, visited Field Marshal Erwin Rommel to give him the chance to commit suicide by poison, rather than facing a public trial from his implication in the plot to assassinate Hitler in July 1944.

Hans-Erich Voss – Continue past Maisel's grave, keeping the edge of the cemetery to your right. Pass nine paths to the left, and just at the hedge on the right, in front of a large building with gray siding outside the cemetery, is the grave of Vice-Admiral Hans-Erich Voss, who served as a naval liaison officer to Hitler's headquarters, was present in the Wolf's Lair conference room when the bomb went off in the attempt on Hitler's life on 20 July 1944, and ended the Second World War in Hitler's Berlin Bunker, an eyewitness to the final scenes of the Third Reich.

Fritz Todt – Take the path that goes into the cemetery (toward the hill) in front of Voss' grave, and then take the first path to the left. At the third path intersection on the right is a large gray marker for the Todt family, including a cenotaph for Fritz Todt, principle constructor of the German *Autobahn* highway system and the fortifications of the West Wall, and Minister of Armaments until his death in a plane crash in 1942. Todt was buried with full military honors in the Invaliden Cemetery in Berlin, but his grave marker was removed by the Soviets after the war. Todt owned a house near here on the Hintersee (see Berchtesgaden Driving Tour No. 5), thus his cenotaph in this Berchtesgaden cemetery.

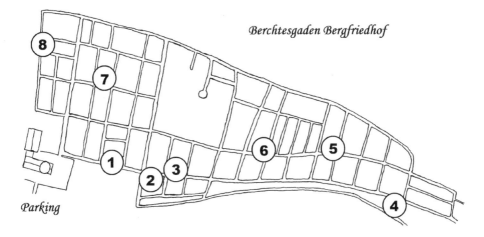

Bergfriedhof – 1. James Kraft, 2. Paula Hitler, 3. Ernst Maisel, 4. Hans-Erich Voss, 5. Fritz Todt, 6. Rudolf Schmundt, 7. Schuster Family, 8. Magda Schneider.

Adolf Hitler's sister Paula is buried in Berchtesgaden, although her name on the grave marker has been covered by a wooden plaque.

Rudolf Schmundt – Continue on this path past the Todt family marker to the fifth path on the right. Beneath a tree at the intersection is a marker for the Schmundt family, including a cenotaph to General Rudolf Schmundt, Adolf Hitler's chief military adjutant, who died of wounds suffered during the assassination attempt on Hitler in July 1944. Schmundt was also buried in the Invaliden cemetery in Berlin, but has a cenotaph here, since his family lived in nearby Markt Schellenberg during the war.

Schuster Family – From Schmundt's marker, take the third path to the right (beside a bench), then the first path to the left. Continue past the second path on the right until you see a large marker for the Familie Schuster, Türken. This is the grave plot of Karl Schuster's family, founder of the Hotel zum Türken on the Obersalzberg (see Obersalzberg Walking Tour No. 2). Schuster himself is not buried here, but the family plot contains the graves of his daughter Therese Partner, who rebuilt the hotel after the bombing damage of 1945, and her daughter Ingrid Scharfenberg, who ran the hotel until her death in 2013.

Magda Schneider – Continue to the end of the path and turn right. Along the hedge on the left side is the grave of actress Magda Schneider, mother of actress Romy Schneider. Magda Schneider owned a house in Schönau near the Königssee lake and was a friend of Adolf Hitler and Eva Braun, who invited her as their guest at the Berghof. Hitler reportedly called Magda Schneider his favorite actress.

Return to the chapel and exit the cemetery (toilets/WC are available down the steps in the back of the chapel). Return in your car to the main street and turn left. At 500 meters (0.3 mile) is a left turn into a parking area for the *Heldenfriedhof* War Graves Cemetery (follow the green sign for *Kriegsgräberstätte*). The War Graves are up a slight rise to your right front (GPS N47.6219, E12.9905, Am Friedhof 24).

Retrace your route to the traffic circle in Berchtesgaden and turn right immediately onto the road to Königssee (B20). In 0.8 km (0.5 mile) turn right toward Schönau. Continue 2.2 km (1.3 miles) and turn left into a driveway just beyond a small chapel; park along the entrance street (GPS N47.6026, E12.9850, Hubertuspark 2). Now called the Hotel Schloss Hubertus, this complex was used during the war as a rest and recreation center for the Luftwaffe; it now fulfills the same purpose for employees of the German railway system. In May 1945 the U.S. 101st Airborne Division consolidated and displayed Hermann Göring's captured art collection here.

Turn right out of the parking area to retrace your route to Berchtesgaden, or turn left and continue on this street (0.7 mile) to visit the Königssee lake area (see Chapter 5).

Actress Magda Schneider visited Adolf Hitler at the Teehaus; on the right is Martin Bormann's wife Gerda.

Theresa Partner, daughter of the original owner of the Hotel zum Türken on the Obersalzberg, rebuilt the house from its ruined condition after the war and managed the hotel for many years along with her daughter Ingrid Scharfenberg.

U.S. Army personnel gathered valuable artworks and stored them for protection here in Berchtesgaden in 1945.

DRIVING TOUR NO. 5

Hintersee – Last Nazi Headquarters in the Area

This tour takes between ninety minutes and two hours. Leave Berchtesgaden to the west on highway B305, following the signs toward Traunstein and Ramsau. At about 8.0 km (5.0 miles) after leaving the Bahnhof, turn left following the sign to Ramsau and Hintersee. When you can see the church ahead, park in the pull-off on the left side, along the river, in the center of Ramsau (GPS N47.6075, E12.8969, across from Im Tal 72). This stop has little to do with Third Reich history, but it is one of the most picturesque views in the area, especially on a sunny day when the mountains can be seen against a blue sky. Walk across the wooden bridge to the Ramsau Malerwinkel ('painters corner'), the spot with the best view for photos and paintings. A visit to the church across the road is also rewarding. The adjacent cemetery has an eye-catching sign over the entrance gate nearest the church, reminding Mankind that he will return to the dust from which he was made. Along the cemetery walls are several memorials to local soldiers who fell on foreign battlefields. Along the wall on the road side, near the church, is an especially interesting and poignant memorial to six soldiers from the Votz family – three brothers who died in the First World War and three brothers who died in the Second World War. This cemetery also has a grave marker for Margret Giesler, wife of Nazi *Gauleiter* (district leader) Paul Giesler, who committed suicide along with his family in the Berchtesgaden area during the final days of the Second World War (the grave marker is on the left side of the main path going through the cemetery).

Continue through Ramsau, following the signs to Hintersee. As the road winds through the woods before the lake, you are passing through the 'Magic Forest' (*Zauberwald*). Angle left toward Hirschbichl. Park in the lot at the end of the road (a pay parking lot) and walk back down the street toward the lake. The first two houses on the right as you walk back are historic structures (GPS for the parking area – N47.5992, E12.8438, Hirschbichlstrasse 22).

House Nr. 11, the *Altes Zollhaus* (Old Customs House), was bought in 1939 by Nazi Minister Fritz Todt. His family lived here during most of the war.

House Nr. 7 is the *Altes Forsthaus* (Old Forestry House). Reichs Minister Hans Lammers moved here from the Chancellery in Stanggass at the end of the war, retreating from advancing Allied forces. One of Hitler's armored Mercedes automobiles was found here by the U.S. 101st Airborne Division (presumably this is the car now on display in the Canadian War Museum in Ottawa).

Return to your car and retrace your route toward the lake. Angle to the left (keeping the lake to your right) and pass the Wörndlhof. Park across the road from Bartel's Gasthof Alpenhof (GPS N47.6043, E12.8494, Am See 27). This guest house, along with the nearby Hotel Post, became the final southern headquarters of the Nazi Party, when Nazi staff adjutant Albert Bormann (brother of *Reichsleiter* Martin Bormann) moved there after the bombing of the Obersalzberg, along with the remaining Berghof staff, Hitler's personal adjutant Julius Schaub, Hitler's secretary Christa Schroeder, Hitler's dentist Prof. Hugo Blaschke, and others. The Alpenhof restaurant serves delicious Bavarian food, and the *Stube* still displays some interesting and surprising wood carvings on the ceiling beams.

Continue along this road and park across from the Gasthaus Seeklause, by the lake (GPS N47.6076, E12.8522, Am See 65). Hitler visited the Seeklause with his press director Otto Dietrich and adjutant Wilhelm Brückner. The adjacent Hotel Post (now the Gästehaus Hintersee) was used to house Third Reich guests during the Nazi period, and refugees from the Obersalzberg in May 1945.

Turn around and retrace your route around the lake, and follow the road signs to return to Berchtesgaden.

Nazi minister Fritz Todt bought this house on the Hintersee lake for his family.

Adolf Hitler visited the Hintersee lake to relax. Hitler is seen here with his press chief Otto Dietrich on the terrace of the Gasthaus Seeklause. The rugged mountains that surround the secluded Hintersee are evident in the background of this view.

Bahnhof Area and Tourist Information Center

This tour takes about twenty minutes. Begin in the main reception hall of the Bahnhof (train station – GPS N47.6262, E13.0000, Bahnhofsplatz 1). (If arriving by car, there is a large parking lot behind the train station, on the other side of the tracks, which you cross via a pedestrian tunnel – see the Hints for Parking in Appendix B.) The mural paintings depicting alpine and Berchtesgaden scenes were done by local artist Maria Harrich in the 1950s, and the large zodiac symbol clock is original to 1937. The monumental style of architecture is typical of Third Reich buildings, which were designed to impress the visitor by their size. Note the original sign above the doorway in back leading to the tracks – *Zu den Zügen* (to the trains). You can see marks that show where similar period signs were mounted in other locations around the hall – at the other end were signs for *Gepäck Expreßgut* (shipped baggage) and *Handgepäck* (hand luggage to check), and in the present bookstore were signs for *Zeitungen* (newspapers), *Andenken* (souvenirs), *Zigarren* (cigars), and *Feinkost* (food, snacks). The bookstore sells several volumes about the Third Reich history of the area, as well as tourism books and maps.

Leave the reception area by the front and turn right outside the station. Notice the large iron flagpoles on the front of the Bahnhof and on adjacent buildings – these poles displayed Nazi banners when Adolf Hitler and other Nazi leaders were present.

Above a wooden door in the courtyard on the right is a period insignia of the *Deutsche Reichsbahn* – the Third Reich period railway service – a winged train wheel. Straight ahead are three stone-framed doorways, which were the original entrance to the Third Reich period post office (today's Burger King restaurant). Above these doorways can be seen a stone wreath which is all that remains of a large eagle and swastika once mounted here.

Walk around to the left of this building to view the famous Berchtesgaden mosaic on the other side. This 1938 mosaic was by the Munich firm of F.X. Zettler, and has been carefully preserved following the removal of the swastika in 1945.

Return to the front entrance of the former post office and pass under the archway marked *Zum Markt / Zentrum*. Climb the fifty steps and turn around at the top to see the date 1937 on the archway above you (the planned start date for building the current Bahnhof).

Return to the front of the Bahnhof and walk past the tower to the entrance with two large stone columns. This was Adolf Hitler's private arrival and departure area when he traveled by train to his Berghof home on the Obersalzberg. Turn around and look across the traffic circle to the building with the dark steeply sloping roof. At the Berchtesgaden area Tourist Information Center (*Kurdirektion*) here, you can get maps and information, arrange lodging, visit restrooms, etc. This building can be seen in the photo showing the Duke of Windsor (former King Edward VIII of Great Britain) and his wife as they were greeted by Nazi Labor Front leader Robert Ley upon their arrival to visit Hitler at the Berghof on 22 October 1937.

A ceremony was held at the Berchtesgaden train station during its construction about 1939.

The Berchtesgaden train station as seen about 1940, after the major construction was completed.

Adolf Hitler had his own special section of the train station, where he could reach his train in privacy.

Above left: A large mosaic featuring a Bavarian holding a Nazi flag appeared on the Berchtesgaden post office.

Above right: The swastika was removed from the flag in 1945, but the mosaic remains otherwise unchanged.

The Duke and Duchess of Windsor were greeted at the train station by Nazi leader Robert Ley (in light overcoat) when they arrived in Berchtesgaden to visit Adolf Hitler.

Main Square, War Memorial, Old Cemetery

This tour takes about forty-five minutes and begins at the *Marktplatz* square in Berchtesgaden (GPS N47.6330, E13.0021, Marktplatz 1). To reach this start point if walking from the bus depot at the train station, make your way up Bahnhofstrasse or down Maximilianstrasse to the *Marktplatz*. If driving, there is no immediately adjacent parking lot, but there are several possibilities for parking in Berchtesgaden (although parking can be limited in town). There is an underground parking garage and several parking lots on Maximilianstrasse. You can also park in the lot beside the Esso fuel station on Bahnhofstrasse and walk up the hill into town (see the Hints for Parking in Appendix B).

Berchtesgaden is a colorful and quaint town surrounded by the Bavarian Alps, whose prosperity has depended for centuries on salt mining and tourism. Germany's third highest mountain, the 2,713 meter (8,901 feet) high Watzmann, towers over the area, and locals like to claim it is actually Germany's highest mountain, as it is the tallest peak that is entirely within Germany's borders. Today, tourists can visit the salt mines and many other scenic and historical sites, and the town can be very crowded during the peak summer tourist season. Berchtesgaden has preserved many old customs, and you may see locals still wearing their traditional *Lederhosen* pants and *Dirndl* dresses as everyday wear, and you may be lucky enough to see a wedding procession or other celebration in full traditional costume.

The Marktplatz was often the scene of Nazi celebrations during the Third Reich period, including gatherings of the *Sturm Abteilung* (SA – Storm Troopers) at the fountain, and a celebration in local costume (*Trachten*) at the Gasthof Neuhaus.

Walk toward the small pedestrian archway to the left of the Gasthof Neuhaus. The small bronze plaque on the right side of this pedestrian archway is a memorial to the victims of the Royal Air Force bombing attack on the Obersalzberg on 25 April 1945. Continue walking through the archways and enter the *Schlossplatz* (Palace Square). Turn around to view the Berchtesgaden war memorial painted over the arcade.

This memorial was originally painted in 1929 by Munich artist Josef Hengge. In June 1945 all but the central figure was painted over as a result of Allied occupation authorities orders to remove all Nazi decorations, even though this memorial was for First World War dead and had nothing to do with the Third Reich. Hengge restored the painting in 1952, adding the dates for the Second World War and changing the right-hand vignette to a less militaristic scene (it originally showed a Wehrmacht soldier with hand grenades, triumphing over fallen Russian soldiers in winter suits). There is also a stone war memorial on the wall inside the arcade area.

The *Schlossplatz* was the scene of the formal surrender of Berchtesgaden to the U.S. Army on 4 May 1945, with the war memorial painting as a backdrop.

Optional – The *Schloss* (Palace), opposite the memorial painting, presents an interesting tour of Berchtesgaden's history from the Romanesque to the 19th century.

Return to the *Marktplatz* (fountain area) and walk downhill, then turn right at the main street (Maximilianstrasse). Walk up this street until you see a garden area (*Kurgarten*) and adjacent cemetery across the street to your left. Cross at the crosswalk and walk along the cemetery wall to the right, toward the church. Walk into the cemetery at the entrance closest to the church.

The local Storm Troopers (SA) group met at the Berchtesgaden fountain in the 1930s.

Above left: The Berchtesgaden market square and fountain provided a subject for a local artist.

Above right: A group of local men in Lederhosen met in front of the Gasthof Neuhaus, festooned with a Nazi flag.

Josef Hengge painted the Berchtesgaden war memorial.

Soldiers of the U.S. 3rd Infantry Division passed the war memorial as they occupied Berchtesgaden.

Berchtesgaden mayor Karl Sandrock (in overcoat) and district commissioner Karl Theodor Jacob (center) surrendered the town to Lieutenant Colonel Kenneth Wallace of the U.S. 3rd Infantry Division on 4 May 1945. Wallace reportedly told the Germans that if a single shot was fired at the Americans, they would pull out of town and the area would be reduced to rubble and ashes by Allied bombers.

Altfriedhof – 1. Anton Adner, 2. 'Moritz' Mayer, 3. Dietrich Eckart, 4. Grethlein and Lohr, 5. Hans Lammers, 6. Richard Voss, 7. Ludwig Hohlwein, 8. Günter Warbeck.

Berchtesgaden's *Altfriedhof* – the Old Cemetery – contains the burial sites of many of the area's most famous figures. Just on the right inside the gate is the grave of Anton Adner, one of the Berchtesgaden area's most famous citizens. Adner was a wood carver and travelling peddler who gained fame and popularity with the Bavarian royalty in his old age, and who lived to be 117 years old.

Walk straight ahead, keeping the church to your right. On the right is a monument for Dr. Moritz Mayer, with a marker at the foot for his granddaughter Mauritia 'Moritz' Mayer, founder of the Pension Moritz on the Obersalzberg, which later became the Platterhof hotel of the Third Reich period (see Obersalzberg Walking Tour No. 1).

Retrace your route to the entry gate and turn right onto the cemetery path that runs beside the wall. Note the soldier memorials, many with photos, along this wall – these memorials were mainly for soldiers who were buried far from Germany, or their remains not otherwise recoverable, or missing. About 110 meters (370 feet) down this path, just past a pathway to the right, is the large grave marker of Dietrich Eckart. Eckart was a nationalist poet and newspaper writer in the early 20th century who became a mentor of Adolf Hitler during his entry into politics. Eckart died in Berchtesgaden in 1923 and was buried here. After the Nazi rise to power in 1933, townspeople who passed Eckart's grave were required to give the raised arm Hitler salute. Apparently his name was removed from the marker at some point (perhaps in 1945) and later re-engraved, as the lettering style is now different from its appearance during the Third Reich.

Just behind Eckart's grave is a marker for Georg Grethlein and Josef Lohr. Grethlein was the leader of one of the engineering firms tasked with the Nazi construction projects on the Obersalzberg. As Allied troops occupied the Obersalzberg on 5 May 1945, Grethlein and his driver Lohr were shot to death by a drunken French soldier, and buried together in this grave.

Anton Adner, one of Berchtesgaden's most famous residents, was pictured in a 1937 Third Reich period tourism brochure. Adner was shown with his peddler's rack on his back, ready for one of his famous excursions through the Bavarian countryside.

Mauritia 'Moritz' Mayer, popularly known as 'Judith Platter', founded the Pension Moritz.

Pension Moritz, Obersalzberg.

Adolf Hitler stayed at the Pension Moritz on the Obersalzberg after his release from prison in 1925.

Above left: Dietrich Eckart's grave in the old Berchtesgaden cemetery was a shrine during the Third Reich period.

Above right: Eckart's grave marker displays his name in slightly different lettering today.

Above left: Georg Grethlein was killed while trying to restore order on the Obersalzberg on 5 May 1945.

Above right: Grethlein's driver Josef 'Sepp' Lohr was also killed by a drunken French soldier.

Continue on the path past the Grethlein/Lohr grave (go past the bench). At the third path to the left is the grave of Reichs Minister Hans-Heinrich Lammers, chief of the Reichs Chancellery (and so boss of the *Kanzlei* complex in Stanggass – see Berchtesgaden Driving Tour No. 1). Although Lammers survived the war, his wife and daughter reportedly committed suicide after being raped by Allied soldiers in the early days of the occupation of Berchtesgaden, and are buried in this same grave.

Walk past the front of Lammers' grave to the cemetery wall and turn left. The third grave on the right is that of Richard Voss (spelled Voß on the marker). Voss was a novelist whose heroine Judith Platter was believed to have been inspired by Mauritia 'Moritz' Mayer of the Pension Moritz on the Obersalzberg. Mayer became popularly known as 'Judith Platter', and after her death her Pension was called the Platterhof (see Obersalzberg Walking Tour No. 1).

The fourth grave on the right past the Voss grave is that of Ludwig Hohlwein, an artist who produced several propaganda posters for the Third Reich (the grave marker is today obscured by two tall cedar trees). Hohlwein also produced the famous monk logo used by the Franziskaner beer brewery. See page 4 for an illustration of one of Hohlwein's posters.

Turn on the path to the left just past Hohlwein's grave. Ten graves up on the left is an interesting marker for the Warbeck family, including a soldier named Günter Warbeck who died on the Russian Front in 1941, and whose grave marker is decorated with an Iron Cross, a helmet, sword, and oak leaves.

Optional – Leave the cemetery by the gate you entered, cross the main street Maximilianstrasse, and walk past the front of the Hotel Watzmann. At the far side of the hotel (on the left) you will see a stairway with 140 steps, leading up to an upper level of the town. At

As chief of the Reichs Chancellery office, Hans-Heinrich Lammers occupied an important and influential government post, both in Berlin and Berchtesgaden. He was a close associate of Adolf Hitler, advising him on various government and legal matters, and he was the boss of the Reichskanzlei complex in Berchtesgaden-Stanggass, responsible for government functions while Hitler was in residence on the Obersalzberg.

An Iron Cross crowns the wartime grave of Günter Warbeck.

Above left: Concrete shelters were positioned at convenient points for the SS guard force.

Above right: This entrance to the 'Berghof' tunnel system is covered by a concrete apron.

the top of this stairway is an intact Moll Bunker, a concrete shelter for military guards during the Third Reich. At the top of the stairway, turn right on Ludwig Ganghofer Strasse and walk down the street as it curves to the left. Just before the main street intersection, on the left you will see a concrete apron covering a tunnel entrance (the entrance is blocked). This was the upper level of the Berghof Tunnel (no relation to Hitler's Berghof home on the Obersalzberg), one of the larger tunnels built in Berchtesgaden as public air raid shelters.

Retrace your route to the *Marktplatz*, or other destination.

(Note – If you have transportation, you can avoid walking up those 140 steps. Park in the pay parking lot at Ludwig Ganghofer Strasse 44 (GPS N47.6295, E12.9986) and walk across the street to the street that angles up the hill on the right (also called Ludwig Ganghofer Strasse, although there is no street sign here). You will see the concrete tunnel entrance on the right, and the Moll Bunker is on up the street on the left, at the top of the stairway.)

Moll Bunkers – These cylindrical concrete shelters designed for two men and produced by the Leonhard Moll company of Munich were placed along guard paths around the Obersalzberg and in Berchtesgaden, as protection from air attacks and bomb shrapnel for the roving SS guard force (they were not meant to be defended or to fight from). Most of these shelters were blown up after the war, and pieces can be seen at many sites around the Obersalzberg. Two intact Moll Bunkers remain on the Obersalzberg (see Obersalzberg Walking Tour No. 5) and one in Berchtesgaden (see Berchtesgaden Walking Tour No. 2).

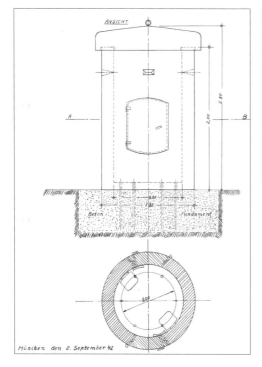

Above: Several air raid tunnels were built in Berchtesgaden. The citizens in the Nonntal district could use this tunnel entrance.

Left: This 1942 plan for a Moll Bunker shows how they were mounted into concrete bases. The section view at bottom shows the two wooden seats for the guards.

CHAPTER 3

Obersalzberg Tours

NOTE: All Obersalzberg driving and walking tours start from the main parking lot for the Kehlsteinhaus (Eagle's Nest) bus ticket office and the Dokumentation Obersalzberg display (pay parking lot), unless otherwise stated (GPS N47.6307, E13.0415, Salzbergstrasse 45). When visiting the Hotel zum Türken Bunker, you can park in the lot behind the hotel (GPS N47.6336, E13.0438, Hintereck 2).

NOTE: Since the American Forces Recreation Center left the Obersalzberg in 1995, and especially since the building of the InterContinental Hotel, changes in roads and parking lots and the Third Reich buildings and ruins themselves have occurred in the area. Doubtless there will be further changes following the publication of this guide book.

NOTE: Many of the areas on the Obersalzberg are now wooded wilderness areas. This guide will tell you how to find the most interesting ruins that are off the beaten path, but please exercise caution when walking in the woods, and especially off the paths. The ruins of the former Nazi buildings are unstable and can be dangerous, and there can be hidden drops into basements – particular caution is advised near the building ruins. The Obersalzberg is a mountain area – good walking shoes, a walking stick or adjustable Nordic walking poles, and appropriate clothing in case of inclement weather are recommended. If you are unused to hiking on steep trails, I recommend taking it slow and easy. If you hike alone, I recommend you notify someone of your destination, and carry a cell/mobile phone with you. Except for the two parts of the underground bunker system that are open to the public, most of the tunnel entrances have been sealed. However, there are some entrances to other underground tunnels that remain open. These tunnels are dangerous and should only be entered at one's own risk. One other bit of advice on two things to avoid when exploring in the woods in the summer – watch out for ticks, which are very common on the Obersalzberg, and stinging nettles (*Brennnesseln*). These are tall slender light green weeds with pointed leaves, that can cause a painful sting even when only slightly touched.

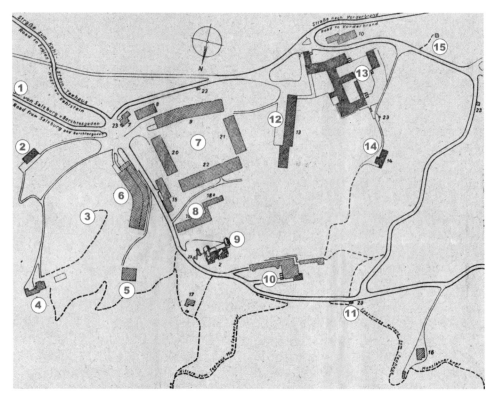

Main sites on the Obersalzberg – 1. coal bunker, 2. Göring Adjutant, 3. InterConti Hotel, 4. Göring, 5. Bormann, 6. greenhouse, 7. SS Barracks, 8. Kindergarten, 9. Türken Hotel, 10. Berghof, 11. SS gate house, 12. Eagle's Nest tickets, 13. Platterhof, 14. Dokumentation, 15. Kampfhäusl

WALKING TOUR NO. I

Platterhof site, Guest House Hoher Göll, Dokumentation Obersalzberg museum, Platterhof bunker, Kampfhäusl

This tour takes between two and two-and-a-half hours, depending on the time spent in the Dokumentation display and bunker. The main Dokumentation/Kehlsteinhaus parking lot occupies the site of the Platterhof hotel (GPS N47.6307, E13.0415). Here in the Pension Moritz, Adolf Hitler first experienced the Obersalzberg when he visited Dietrich Eckart in early 1923. The original guest house, parts of which dated back to the seventeenth century, was converted by the Nazis into the large Platterhof hotel in 1938. The hotel was meant to house the many visitors who came to see Hitler's home in the mid-1930s, but by the time it was finished, security concerns kept these visitors away from the Obersalzberg and the hotel never fulfilled its original purpose.

The occupying American military force reopened the building in 1952 as the General Walker Hotel, one of the main hotels of the American Forces Recreation Center. After the AFRC left Berchtesgaden in 1995, the Platterhof/Walker Hotel was unused, and it was torn down in 2000. The only remains of the Platterhof that can be seen today are the arcades now housing souvenir shops, the side Terrace Hall (which was modified around 1955 by the AFRC, and is now the

The Platterhof hotel was a large complex that occupied today's parking area.

Berggasthof Obersalzberg restaurant), and the stone stairways and terraces. Walk down the stone staircase beside the Terrace Hall (present restaurant) and observe the dates 1854 and 1591 cut into the rocks on the side – these are said to be stones from buildings originally on this site.

The Dokumentation Obersalzberg display occupies the remains of the Guest House Hoher Göll, which was used by *Reichsleiter* Martin Bormann to house Nazi Party administration offices and occasional high ranking guests (GPS N47.6315, E13.0403, Salzbergstrasse 41). The Guest House (which was originally three stories) remained on the site in a ruined condition until 1999, when it was rebuilt to house this display. The only remaining original parts of the Guest House are the entry arches and part of the basement. From the basement you can enter part of the Obersalzberg air raid shelter and tunnel/bunker system. There is an entrance fee to the museum (discounted with a *Kurkarte*, student ID, or military ID), which includes entry into the bunker. Note that the Dokumentation center can be very crowded at times from school and tourist groups, and it can be quite warm in the summer. The display labels are not in English, but an English audio guide is available. For those who are primarily interested in the history of the Obersalzberg in the Third Reich, I recommend the upper floor of the display and the bunker/tunnel system in the basement, as the remainder of the museum is concerned mainly with general Second World War, Holocaust, and political history (a planned expansion, scheduled to be complete by 2018, will have more displays on the history of the Obersalzberg).

The tunnel system reached from the basement was an air raid shelter for the personnel of the Platterhof hotel and the Nazi Party functionaries working in the Guest House, as well as medical personnel from the military hospital that operated in the Platterhof from 1943–1945.

The dates 1591 and 1854 are from older buildings previously on this site.

The Platterhof complex escaped heavy damage during the 1945 bombing attacks, and was renovated into a recreation center for the American military.

Eva Braun (right) and her friend Herta Schneider walked past a guard house in front of the Hoher Göll Guest House. Eva and Herta had been best friends since their youth, and when Eva became Hitler's mistress and the 'lady' of the Berghof, Herta often visited there with her two children. During the Second World War she and her children lived with Eva at the Berghof or in Munich, since Herta's husband was a soldier at the front. Also seen in this view is one of Eva's black Scottish terriers, named Negus and Stasi.

Its primary entrance was from the basement of the Platterhof hotel, and it was planned to have a staircase and/or elevator in a shaft connecting to Adolf Hitler's Berghof tunnel and an SS tunnel at lower levels (you can see this shaft at the end of one of the tunnel hallways). The tunnel doorway where you entered served both as an emergency exit and an entry for personnel in the Guest House. Hint – Although the museum above can be hot in the summer, the tunnel is always cool and a light jacket is recommended. A hand flashlight can be useful to view details in some of the darker tunnel passages.

Shortly after the tunnel entrance is a branch to the right which is the main passageway today. The unfinished area straight ahead (behind the plexiglass tunnel map, which shows the major tunnel systems in the central Obersalzberg area) was planned for an air lock against gas attacks and machine gun positions to guard the entrance, but these were not installed. As you pass down the corridor to the right, notice at the archway how these tunnels were constructed: a layer of cement against the rock, then a layer of black rubber-like waterproofing material, then layers of bricks, and finally the finish layer of cement. These tunnels were built by workers from Germany, Italy, Czechoslovakia, and other European countries, under the direction of a special unit of SS tunnel construction experts. The tunnel plans had to take into account the underlying geology, as well as drainage and emergency exit possibilities.

In the next room past the archway, the open area in the floor (behind a railing) was a fuel tank for the electrical generators, which were housed in the large chamber just ahead. Two large diesel generators were mounted on the concrete pedestals on the floor beneath the modern walkway. These generators provided primary and backup power for the entire central Obersalzberg tunnel system, including the air raid shelters for Hitler and Bormann and the air defense control center. Look on the right side near the iron brackets projecting from the wall,

59

Above left: The original entrance to the tunnel system was down this staircase from the basement of the Platterhof hotel.

Above right: Today's tunnel entrance was originally an emergency exit, seen here in 1945.

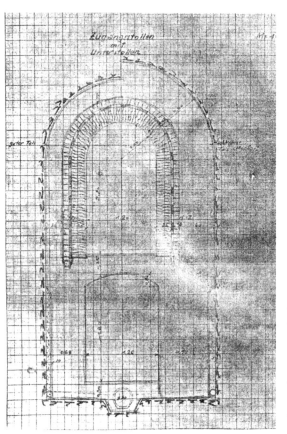

Original construction plans showed the two level design of the main tunnel systems. The passageway on top was lined with concrete, brick, and waterproof sheeting, and was used as the main personnel passageway. Beneath this in most of the tunnels was a second, smaller, passageway, for heating, ventilation, and water pipes, electrical conduits, and other support apparatus. At the bottom were pipes to carry away the ground water and waste water.

and you will see lettering '2 DB. AG. PS. DA. 5.5.1945'. This was scratched into the wall by one of the first Allied soldiers to reach the Obersalzberg on 5 May 1945, a member of the French 2nd Armored Division. Near this marking is a construction worker's diagram showing planned electrical installation in the tunnel wall (similar markings can be seen in various other places around this tunnel). You will also see a great deal of other graffiti inscriptions in this tunnel system, but most were scratched by tourists after these tunnels were opened to the public in the 1950s.

If you turn left leaving the generator chamber, you will pass a kitchen/larder and office chambers for Martin Bormann's Party Chancellery (which was housed in the Guest House). One of these chambers still has a large metal wall safe lying in the floor since 1945. You can see smoke stains on the ceiling and walls of the other room (and other chambers further on), where Nazi Party documents were burned at the end of the war to keep them from falling into Allied hands. Toward the end of this passageway you can look to the left back through the unfinished air lock corridor, toward the doorway where you entered from the Guest House basement. At the end of this passageway is an unfinished shaft that led to a tunnel system for the SS Barracks and Hitler's Berghof tunnel system, located lower in the mountain. On the right is a toilet room. In the floor of this passageway (back the way you came) is a hole exposing the *Unterstollen* or lower tunnel for piping, air circulation, and electrical cables.

Retrace your route to where you turned out of the large generator hall, and continue straight ahead in this passageway. The rooms to the left of this hallway were used mainly as air raid shelter rooms for the military convalescent hospital that was established in the Platterhof in 1943. The room on the right of this hallway still contains original ventilation equipment and pipes.

At the end of this hallway is an unfinished chamber that would have had air locks against gas attacks and machine gun positions guarding the original entrance and a planned emergency exit. The boring in the rock at the end was this emergency exit tunnel in progress. On the left side of this chamber you can look down through a break in the floor to see into the piping tunnel beneath this level. On the right side you can see rusting remains of the gas filters for the ventilation system that would have been installed here (large cylindrical drums), as well as other artifacts left since 1945. At the end of the hallway on the left is a machine gun position guarding the stairway that was the original entrance from the Platterhof basement. The rusted iron object on the floor is a machine gun mount like those in position in the concrete tunnel wall.

Retrace your route down the hallway and turn right opposite the large generator chamber, into the Video and Audio rooms. Both of these presentations are in German, but the 38-minute video is well worth the time (copies of this film can be purchased at the ticket counter at the museum entrance). Go straight out of the Audio/Video Room, through the generator chamber, and out the tunnel exit to return through the Dokumentation center to the main parking lot. From the parking lot you can walk to the bus ticket office for the Kehlsteinhaus (Eagle's Nest) tour – the ticket office occupies the site of the Platterhof employee housing building and garage (the ruins were torn down in 2000). (See Chapter 4)

To visit the site of the Kampfhäusl, the small cabin where Adolf Hitler wrote the second part of his book *Mein Kampf* in 1925, return to the main parking area and cross the road directly across from the upper level of the Berggasthof Restaurant to a large yellow road sign. About seven meters (23 feet) downhill from the sign, take the small path that goes off to the left, above

The air filtrations systems were designed by the Dräger company of Lübeck. The system seen here was found intact beneath the Berchtesgadener Hof hotel.

Above left: Hitler used a small wooden cabin to complete his book *Mein Kampf.*

Above right: The 'Kampfhäusl' cabin was over watched by a 'Moll Bunker' guard shelter like this one.

the sidewalk, toward the woods. Enter the woods on this path and continue about 110 meters (360 feet) – the road will be below you to the right. The rock foundation of the Kampfhäusl will be visible in the woods, just uphill to the left. The cabin was only slightly damaged during the April 1945 bombing attack but was torn down around 1952. Remains of a broken-up Moll Bunker guard shelter that was located behind the cabin can be seen around the foundation site (GPS N47.6299, E13.0396). Hitler did not actually live in this cabin, but only used it during the day as a writer's retreat. During this period, Hitler lived at the Platterhof pension, and later in various hotels in Berchtesgaden itself.

WALKING TOUR NO. 2

Hotel zum Türken Bunker Tour and Adolf Hitler's Berghof Home

This tour takes about ninety minutes. Park in the lot behind the Hotel zum Türken (GPS N47.6336, E13.0438, Hintereck 2) and enter the Bunker tour at the kiosk at the rear of the hotel (there is an entrance fee). This bunker tour is self-guided (you can buy a map and explanation in English at the kiosk before you enter the Bunker), and leads through several levels to SS prisoner cells, machine gun nests, a bunker emergency exit, and the entrance to Hitler's Berghof tunnel system (the Berghof tunnel itself is closed to the public). Note: this tour contains several stairways covering four levels with 125 steps total – climbing the stairs back to the surface can be strenuous, and the underground passages can be slippery. The tunnels are cold and damp, much like a natural cave, so I recommend a jacket. I also recommend a small flashlight, as some of the passageways are rather dimly lit.

At the kiosk turnstile, insert the proper change or token and push the turnstile in one motion (don't stop – if you stop pushing partway through, it will require another payment). The spiral staircase was a postwar addition – this was not the original entryway to the tunnel. Turn left at the first landing and pass the toilets. Ahead of you are SS prisoner cells in the basement of the hotel, used for punishment for minor infractions. The walls are painted black to simulate their appearance after the war, as these rooms were smoke blackened during the bombing in 1945.

Proceed to the bottom of the staircase and through the original entrance to this tunnel. As the route cuts through the brick archway note how the original passageways were built up in different layers, including black rubberlike waterproof sheeting. In the hallway you can see mounts for electrical and telephone cables and water pipes along the walls, and a passage for air ducts beneath the floor. At the end of the hallway, the left turn led to Martin Bormann's tunnel system and the air defense command center. This tunnel is blocked several feet on, as it passes beneath the road outside the Hotel zum Türken parking lot. The right turn leads you further into the tunnel system.

The Türken tunnel system was not intended as an actual air raid shelter, but was called a *Verbindungsstollen* – a connecting tunnel. Bormann had this tunnel built so he could pass underground between his tunnel system and the tunnel system of Adolf Hitler's Berghof house – the Türken just happened to be located between. Although they are often called Bunkers today, the Obersalzberg tunnel systems were not actually designed as defensive fortifications, but only as air raid shelters. The entries were guarded by machine guns for defense against limited attacks such as a raid by a small force of paratroopers or special forces, not against prolonged assaults or a siege.

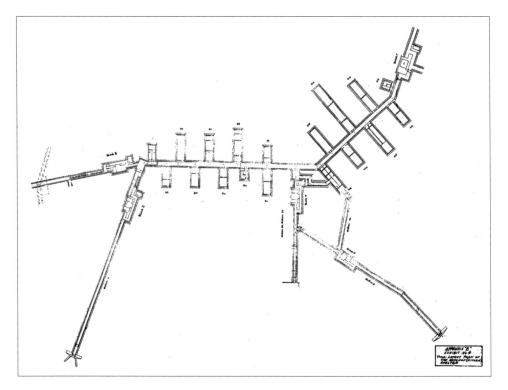

Hitler's Berghof tunnel was completed in three sections. The part that can be visited from the Hotel zum Türken today is outlined in red.

The long staircase was necessary since the level of Hitler's tunnel system was lower in the mountain than Bormann's. At the bottom of the staircase you can see the first of several machine gun positions. These guarded the entrances with right-angle passageways, so an enemy could not fire directly into the tunnel hallways. There are three machine gun nests here, guarding both directions of travel. For further security, these machine gun positions can only be entered from the level below this one (you will see this later in the tour). Note that on this side, the holes for the machine guns and for viewing are built up in steps, not as a flat sloping surface. This was to catch enemy bullets on the steps, so they would not ricochet into the openings.

Leave the machine gun positions and walk toward the open area – you can see where a metal bunker door was once mounted, as well as anti-gas vents above the doorways (labeled *Gas-Schleuse*). These vents worked by overpressure of the air from the tunnel ventilation equipment, which kept air flowing out of the tunnels through these vents so that gas could not enter when the bunker doors were sealed. In the event that the ventilation system wasn't working, the gas vents closed to prevent air from flowing the other way into the tunnels. Hitler was particularly fearful of gas attacks, since he had been wounded in the First World War by mustard gas.

On the right is a kennel for guard dogs (*Hundezwinger*) – a sign on the wall notes that here you are about 70 meters (230 feet) underground. Walk straight ahead to the bricked up doorway with the gas vent above it – this doorway continued on to the Berghof tunnel system, with comfortable rooms for Adolf Hitler, his mistress Eva Braun, his doctor Theodor Morell, and other staff. The doorway is bricked up because Hitler's tunnel is not open to the public, but if you hold a small camera up to the opening at the top left of the bricks, you may get a photo looking down the hallway into Hitler's tunnel.

On the left are break rooms, toilets, and a shower for the SS guard personnel. Return to the open area and take the stairway straight ahead. Both stairways lead to the same lower level, which was for ventilation and other machinery, and was also guarded by machine gun positions.

At the bottom of the steps, turn left into the open area. Ventilation machinery was originally mounted in the room on the right. In this area you can see mounts for electrical cables on the walls and ceilings. The large room ahead contains original ventilation ducting. The bricked up doorway leads to the lower level of the Berghof tunnel (this is beneath the bricked up doorway on the level above you). Most of the main Obersalzberg tunnel systems were built with two levels – the main level for shelter during an air raid, and the lower level for ventilation machinery and ducting, plumbing, cables, etc.

Turn around and pass the stairs you came down, following the sign for *MG-Stände*. On the right, and on down this hallway, you will see three rooms with metal rung ladders and circular openings in the ceiling – this was the access to the machine gun positions that you saw on the level above. The access to these elaborate positions was made through the floor so that an attacker could not force the defender out of a machine gun room on its own level.

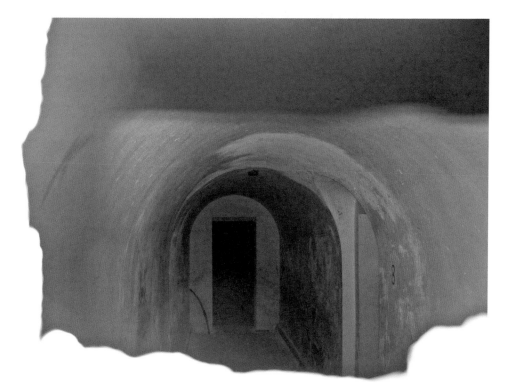

Hitler's tunnel system is still intact beyond the brick doorway.

At the end of the hallway (where a flashlight is useful), and along the wall, you can see the results of decades of water flowing down the walls and vents. Much like a natural cave, 'flowstone' from dissolved calcite and other minerals has built up on the walls and has mostly blocked the cable and ventilation shafts at this end.

Return past the machine gun positions and turn right in the machinery room. Walk down the hallway marked *MG-Stand*. Walk straight ahead through the narrow doorway – you are now inside the machine gun position on the left, where you can see the metal rails for mounting the weapon and the handle for closing the metal port shutter (the viewport here has been blocked).

Continue to the machine gun position at the end of the hallway. The damage you see here is said to have been caused by an explosive bazooka round that was fired by a U.S. soldier in 1945 through the tunnel emergency exit that is on the other side. Whether such a shot would have been likely in this cramped area is debatable, but in any case you can see the effect of high explosives on the steel-reinforced concrete of these tunnel walls.

Turn around and return to the main hallway, turn right, and then right again. At the end of the passageway you are now on the other side of the damaged machine gun position. The bazooka was supposedly fired from the dark hallway which led out through an emergency exit into the valley in front of the Berghof (closed today). If you brought a flashlight, you may be able to see the metal bunker door at the end of the exit hallway. All of these air raid shelter tunnels had emergency exits on a different level and at some distance from the normal entrance, for use in case the entrance was blocked as a result of a bombing attack, or to escape in case the main entrance was breached by an enemy.

Retrace your route and take the stairway on the right, following the *Ausgang* (Exit) signs. Note the original metal handrail. At the top of the steps, turn left and go through the doorway marked *Gas-Schleuse* above. Continue to follow the *Ausgang* signs to the stairways leading up and out. The final staircase has 61 steps, but there is a landing partway up where you can stop for a rest. The hallway that turns left past these stairs leads to the spiral staircase and exit at the kiosk.

From the parking lot you can view the side of the Hotel zum Türken and a guard house for the SS guard placed at the entrance to the inner Führer area (Hitler's house was just down the road from here). The hotel is private property, so please respect the signs restricting photography and access to the front terrace. The original building here dated to the seventeenth century, when it was owned by a veteran of the Habsburg wars with the Ottoman Turks, who was himself called the 'Turk'. The 'Little Turk House' was built into a hotel in 1911 and operated as such until the owner was forced to move out in 1933, and the building was taken over by the Nazi Security Service (RSD – *Reichssicherheitsdienst* – not the Gestapo, as is often stated). In practice, this house was used by Adolf Hitler's personal body guards and the SS guard force who rotated among the posts in the inner Führer area, including Hitler's house. The Türken was badly bombed and completely plundered in April-May 1945, but the original owner's family rebuilt the ruins and reopened the hotel in the 1950s.

Allied soldiers damaged the bunker walls with high explosives in 1945.

The emergency exit to the tunnel beneath the Hotel zum Türken was closed by a simple metal bunker door. This exit and the other exit to the Berghof tunnel system would have had two doors, another one a few feet beyond this one. The bunker doors had seals to hinder the entry of poison gases or smoke from exploding bombs, but the filter systems inside the tunnels themselves would have served as the main prevention of incoming gas or smoke.

In the early 1930s crowds gathered at the Hotel zum Türken to catch a glimpse of Hitler at his adjacent house.

The Türken served as the Obersalzberg headquarters for Hitler's personal security detachment.

The 1945 bombing attack severely damaged the Türken building, and the ruins were sometimes confused with Hitler's house, since some soldiers were apparently expecting to see the old wooden chalet 'Haus Wachenfeld'.

Adolf Hitler's Berghof Home

To visit the site of Hitler's Obersalzberg home, leave the Hotel zum Türken parking lot and walk down the hill to the left on the main road (watching for traffic – some folks drive pretty fast on these mountain roads). Just below the Türken is a path leading uphill to the left – this path follows the auxiliary Berghof driveway and leads to the site. As you reach the trees, the main part of the Berghof was just in front of you (GPS N47.6337, E13.0416).

The most striking visible remainder of the Berghof is the concrete retaining wall that ran along the back of the house (parts of the basement remain but are inaccessible). The famous terrace was on top of the garage (no longer standing), toward the front of the site, before the slope. Hitler chose this location as a home partly for the view – he could look north to his native Austria (Salzburg is visible in the cleft between the mountains to the right front), and to the magnificent Untersberg mountain range, where legend says Charlemagne was buried.

As you walk around the Berghof site, especially along the retaining wall, keep your eyes open for small strips of green or brown plastic. These are pieces of the camouflage nets that were hung across the Obersalzberg buildings toward the end of the Second World War in an unsuccessful attempt to disguise them from aerial reconnaissance. The plastic strips were originally attached to wire netting in bundles, but the parts that remain today are generally just small broken pieces of the plastic strips.

Hitler initially lived in a small wooden mountain chalet here, which he first rented in 1928 (according to his own recollections) and then purchased in 1933. This 'Haus Wachenfeld' proved too small for Hitler as a world leader, so it was enlarged in 1936 into the grandiose

Hitler's Berghof consisted of a main house, an attached side wing, and a detached wing for adjutants and support personnel (on the other side of the house).

Today's access path leads to the site of the side wing shown in this period painting.

The concrete retaining wall can be seen behind the house in this 1938 postcard.

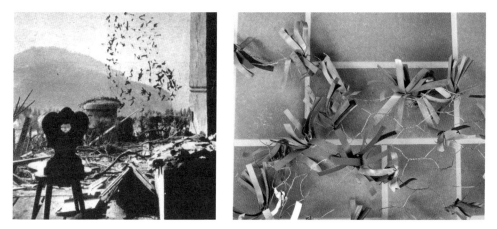

Above left: Camouflage netting was hung from the Obersalzberg buildings. A 'Moll Bunker' guard shelter is seen in the background.

Above right: The camouflage netting on the Obersalzberg buildings was made from strips of green and brown plastic attached to a wire base. Although the wire netting has disappeared in most areas, pieces of the green and brown plastic strips are commonly found around the Obersalzberg ruins sites today. Aerial photographs taken in 1945 show that the camouflage nets were not a deterrent to Allied reconnaissance.

'Berghof' mansion, partly based on Hitler's own design plans. Although Hitler had a residence in Berlin as German Chancellor, and also owned an apartment in Munich, the Berghof was his home, and he spent as much time here in his adopted Obersalzberg homeland as possible. Many of Hitler's plans for political and military domination, which affected millions of people during the Second World War, were made here at the Berghof.

During the Royal Air Force bombing attacks of 25 April 1945, the Berghof area was hit by several bombs and the house itself was badly damaged. Just before abandoning the area, the SS guards set fire to the ruins, and little but a burned-out shell remained to be captured by American soldiers on 4 May 1945. The ruins were finally blown up and covered in April 1952. In the years since, trees have grown up and several feet of fill dirt and rubble have been added across the site, especially along much of the retaining wall, obscuring most details that remained of this historic site.

It takes an active imagination to picture this site as it looked when Hitler lived here. As you stand in front of the information marker, you are standing about where the Berghof was built onto the old Haus Wachenfeld, near the doorway between Haus Wachenfeld and the Berghof. The famous picture window at the front of the Great Room would have been a short distance to your right front, with the grand staircase to the right of that, and the garage with terrace on the roof was about the same distance to your left front (the garage ruin was removed in 1995).

The open area to the left of the information marker was the site of a patio just outside the Berghof winter garden (sunroom), behind the garage terrace and in front of the Adjutancy wing. This patio was a favorite gathering area for the Berghof inner circle and regular guests of Hitler, where Eva Braun and her friends liked to sun themselves on reclining chairs.

If you take the paths that lead downhill to either side just behind the marker, to the left you can see a concrete strip and some stone foundations that mark the base of the garage at its front. To the right you can see some of the original asphalt driveway. This is near the bottom of the grand staircase where Hitler's state visitors arrived in Mercedes limousines and where Hitler himself often greeted them. Following this path through the woods downhill leads to the main driveway entrance where Hitler stood to recognise his crowds of followers as they marched past on the road below the Hotel zum Türken in the 1930s. Martin Bormann had a linden tree planted here to give Hitler some shade in the summer. The tree was cut down in the 1960s, but shoots bearing distinctive linden leaves still grow up there (GPS N47.63392, E13.04245).

Return to the upper area by the marker. The entrance to Hitler's air raid shelter tunnel was in the retaining wall near the back corner in the middle, but it is now buried by fill and rubble. The brick-lined opening just above the retaining wall on the western side (around the curved part, behind what was the Berghof Adjutancy staff office wing) was a conduit for communications cables. Continuing along the path past the western side of the site leads one to the Guest House and Dokumentation Obersalzberg.

Several small paths lead off into the weeds at the front of the site, on the side where the retaining wall is lower (where the Berghof Adjutancy was located). These paths lead down the hillside to the left, and eventually to one of the emergency exits to Hitler's air raid shelter tunnel system. This exit – not the one you saw in the Türken tunnel – is closed today. The path also leads past the remains of a curved concrete wall that bordered a small alpine garden below this wing of the Berghof. Near here on the slope you can see moss-covered pieces of a Moll Bunker concrete guard shelter that once stood above near the Adjutancy, but that was blown up after the war.

Hitler improved Haus Wachenfeld by adding a garage, sunroom, and terrace in 1933.

An aerial reconnaissance photo taken shortly after the bombing attack shows three direct bomb hits on the Berghof with several near misses. The retaining wall along the back of the house is clear in this photo.

The showpiece of Hitler's Berghof was the Great Room with picture window.

Furniture was arranged around the red marble fireplace in the Berghof.

The Berghof was decorated with costly artworks and tapestries.

Atop the Berghof garage was a cozy sun terrace.

Hitler's original Haus Wachenfeld had a magnificent view of the Untersberg mountains to the north.

Haus Wachenfeld was a small rustic mountain chalet when Hitler first moved in.

These men built a scale model of Haus Wachenfeld using 63,000 wooden matches, which took them thirteen months or 2,160 hours to complete.

During construction in 1936, Haus Wachenfeld was dwarfed by the massive brick and stone walls of the Berghof.

The SS guards at the Hotel Türken had this view of their boss's house next door.

The Berghof dining hall was decorated with costly pine wall paneling.

The April 1945 bombing attack and subsequent fire left the Berghof in ruins. The author's father took this photograph when he visited in the spring of 1946.

Today, visitors to the Berghof site can see only the retaining wall that stood in back of the building and a few smaller artifacts.

Adolf Hitler and Eva Braun walked their dogs beside the Berghof in June 1942.

Berghof guests sunned themselves outside the sunroom. Left–right: Gretl Braun (Eva's sister), actress Else von Möllendorff, Martin Bormann's wife Gerda, Herta Schneider (Eva's best friend).

The original garage was replaced when Haus Wachenfeld was expanded into the Berghof in 1936. The new garage used red marble blocks from the nearby Untersberg mountain. Fumes from the garage reportedly seeped into the Berghof when the large picture window just above the entry was open.

The shade tree planted by Martin Bormann is seen here at the right of the driveway.

The Berghof driveway is mostly buried today.

Gretl Braun (left) took tea on the Berghof terrace with diplomat Walter Hewel and military adjutants, with the wooden Adjutancy wing in the background.

This emergency exit to Hitler's tunnel system would allow personnel to escape down the road toward Berchtesgaden.

The white concrete wall at the right side of this front view of the Berghof is the low curved wall that you stepped over.

This 'Moll Bunker' (with camouflage netting on the top) was blown up after the war, and pieces can be seen on the slope below the Berghof site.

The Berghof garage was situated to the front and side of the main building.

SS Kaserne Site, Greenhouse Ruins, Hintereck Area, Bormann's House Site, Göring's House Site, Adjutant's House, Coal Bunker

This tour takes about an hour. Walk uphill on the sidewalk behind the Hotel zum Türken. Directly across the road is an opening to a tunnel system for the air defense control center (this tunnel is not open to the public). Further up on the right you will pass the sites of a large Kindergarten building and a smaller building to store films and architectural models, and further on, the location of the SS Kaserne (Barracks). The site of the SS Kaserne is the large sunken open area to the right, beyond the pedestrian overpass, where a pond is located today. The Obersalzberg SS Kaserne consisted of four large buildings: a barracks building, mess hall and administration building, a modern gymnasium with a parquet wood floor, and a motor pool building for military trucks and the various automobiles used to transport the Nazi hierarchy and visitors. A smaller adjacent building housed the vehicle drivers, and a nearby building served as offices for the Obersalzberg administration staff. The SS Kaserne was badly damaged during the 1945 bombing and the major building ruins were removed in 1952. Although the building floors and basements remained, as well as an underground shooting range, these ruins were removed from 2001 to 2002.

As you continue up the road beyond the site of the SS Kaserne, you can see the Eagle's Nest on the mountain to your right front. The level area here at the top of the road from the Hotel zum Türken is called Hintereck. This was the center of the Obersalzberg community prior to the Nazi takeover. Martin Bormann had the homes and buildings here torn down before the SS Kaserne was built.

Turn left into the parking area past the end of the rock wall, before the hotel entrance. What appears to be a curving concrete wall on the right is actually the ruin of the greenhouse that Martin Bormann had built to cater to Hitler's vegetarian diet (GPS N47.6329, E13.0456). What you see are the remains of the two-story back wall which supported the metal frames for the greenhouse glass roof and windows, as well as water pipes for irrigation.

Continue past the end of the greenhouse foundation, until you see a yellow metal pole (gas line marker) on the left. A tunnel runs under the sidewalk just beneath the end of the greenhouse, and the entrance to this tunnel is located in the hillside below the yellow pole (the entrance can be seen by taking the path that goes downhill just before the pedestrian bridge – the entrance is in the woods just to the left of the yellow pole above). Continuing past the yellow gas line marker, Bormann's own house was located just ahead to the left, in the area where a ski lift hut now stands (GPS N47.6341, E13.0452). Bormann's house was badly damaged by the April 1945 bombing attack, and the ruins were demolished in 1952.

Continue on this path to the rear of the InterContinental Hotel. As you walk along, the underground anti-aircraft command center and Bormann's tunnel system are beneath the hotel building to your right. There is a marker on the right at the end of the path which commemorates the capture of the Obersalzberg by the U.S. 3rd Infantry Division in May 1945. This marker was placed here by veterans of the 3rd Infantry Division on the anniversary in 2008. Look up and take in the magnificent mountain view to the north – this is one of the reasons why the Obersalzberg was and is so popular.

An American soldier guards the tunnel entrance across the road from the Türken in 1945.

The SS Barracks complex comprised several buildings in 1941.

The greenhouse was originally only one story, and had an adjacent building where mushrooms were grown.

The children who lived on the Obersalzberg enjoyed Easter egg hunts in the greenhouse. The white wall on the right is the concrete wall that you see today.

American soldiers found the greenhouse glass and metal shattered in May 1945.

The entrance to a short tunnel is located near the site of Martin Bormann's house.

The purpose and original destination of this tunnel are unclear today.

Martin Bormann renovated an existing house into a luxury residence for his family on the Obersalzberg. Bormann and his wife Gerda had ten children, who had spacious bedrooms, a small swimming pool, and play areas such as the nearby greenhouse. The basement had an entry into Bormann's personal air raid tunnel system, complete with kitchens, baths, office space, store rooms, and bedrooms for the family and staff.

The 1945 bombing attack reduced Bormann's house to ruins. His family took shelter in the air raid tunnel beneath.

Turn on the curving path toward the children's play area behind the hotel. Reichs Marshal Hermann Göring's house was located on the far side of the InterContinental Hotel, where there is now a pond to the right of the path. There are no remains of Göring's house today, but his air raid shelter is beneath the hillside in this area (GPS N47.6348, E13.0471). Walk up the small hill just ahead, where there is a bench beneath the trees. Directly behind this bench area are some stone steps, the only reminders of Göring's property here.

Return to the path signpost at the edge of the cobblestone walkway.

Optional – If you wish to visit the emergency exit doorway to Göring's air raid tunnel, turn right on the gravel path that angles downhill and into the woods, following the yellow sign that says 'InterContinental Rundweg'. The tunnel emergency exit is about a seven minute walk along this path, on the right (the tunnel itself is not open to the public). Be advised that the path is all downhill, so it is all uphill walking back, but a gentle slope. The metal door that you see at the tunnel exit was installed after the war, when the large arched opening was partly filled with masonry (in common with most of the tunnel exits on the Obersalzberg). Return to the path intersection behind the InterContinental Hotel.

Continue on the cobblestone walkway behind the hotel, walking just behind the pond where Göring's house was located. When the path ends, continue downhill to the left beside the hotel driveway. A short distance on the left is a gravel path with a wooden sign for the *Falknerei/Tiergehege* (Falconry/Animal Sanctuary). You can follow this gravel path as it winds down the hillside, or if you wish, you can continue downhill beside the hotel driveway and turn left at the end, then walk through the parking area.

Hitler watched as Göring practiced archery in front of his house. The small wooded hill in the background can still be seen.

Göring had one of the best views of the area mountains from his house.

The Göring family took shelter from the 1945 bombs in their own air raid tunnels, which exited here behind the house.

The white three-story building below the path was the home and office of General Karl Bodenschatz, Göring's adjutant and liaison officer to Hitler's staff (GPS N47.6330, E13.0480, Hintereck 9). The building is practically unchanged and is now a private residence (please do not trespass on the property).

Optional – Continuing on this path leads to the Falconry and Animal Enclosure (some signs also call it the *Adler und Murmeltiergehege*), an open-air sanctuary and zoo for indigenous birds of prey and *Murmeltiere*, the charming alpine marmots. Don't let the unusual decorations above the entrance gate deter you – the unique exhibit inside is very popular with children, who can sometimes feed the *Murmeltiere*. There are also signs along the paths which point out bomb craters and large pieces of bomb shrapnel from the 25 April 1945 attack. (No set entrance fee – donations are welcome.)

Walk back through the parking lot to the main road and turn left. In about 120 meters (380 feet), follow the partially paved driveway that angles up into the woods on the right. You will pass a closed entrance to an underground tunnel system on the right – this led to shelters for the Hintereck inhabitants and those living in the Klaushöhe settlement. Further along this path is the *Koksbunker*, or coal depot (GPS N47.6318, E13.0494). This massive building held 10,000 cubic meters (over 3,500 tons) of coal for the Obersalzberg central heating system. Trucks delivered the coal through openings in the top (there is another road at the upper level), then smaller trucks pulled into these doorways and filled up from the main supply hoppers above, to deliver their loads to various Obersalzberg buildings. The coal bunker was set on fire in May 1945, either by retreating SS troops or by Allied soldiers, and the contents reportedly smoldered for five months! NOTE: Do not enter the coal bunker – the interior is deteriorating and can be dangerous!

Göring's adjutant and staff had a large building dedicated to service of the Reichs Marshal.

The hillside behind the coal bunker contains an air raid shelter tunnel system.

As you return back down the path, to your right you will see three period buildings on the other side of the road. These Hintereck housing units were built in 1938 for Obersalzberg administration personnel (these are also private residences now – no trespassing, please). There was originally a fourth building here, but it was bombed in 1945 and its ruins were torn down around 1952.

Retrace your route to the start point.

WALKING TOUR NO. 4

Over the Bodnerbichl Hill to the Berghof Site

This tour takes about an hour and leads to several ruins and artifacts that can be found in the woods on the hill above the site of Hitler's Berghof house. Start at the Dokumentation Obersalzberg parking lot, near the stairs leading down to the Kehlsteinhaus (Eagle's Nest) bus ticket office. Walk uphill on the path just outside the line of trees, near the P1 parking lot sign. Leave the path as it curves away from the woods and skirt the woodline, then enter the woods directly ahead (as you enter the woods you are on a broad path that was once a Third Reich roadway).

Proceed approximately sixty meters until you come to the concrete door of a Moll Bunker guard shelter. This Moll Bunker sat near the top of the Bodnerbichl hill, and was blown up after the war. Angle up the hill to the left here, following the 'trail' of concrete pieces until you get to the moss-covered circular top of the Moll Bunker. Among some tree trunks near one of the concrete pieces you can see rusted remains of the chain-link security fence that surrounded the Inner Führer Area here, which was patrolled by the SS guard force. Turn left here and walk uphill, passing a large side piece of the bunker, until you get to the path on top of the hill, and turn right.

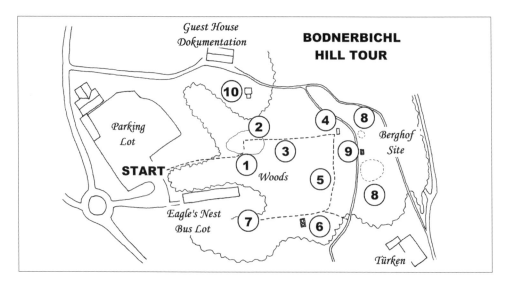

Bodnerbichl Hill – 1. 'Moll Bunker', 2. siren, 3. cable shaft, 4. water cistern, 5. cable shaft, 6. water reservoir, 7. rubble, 8. bomb craters, 9. Berghof reservoir, 10. tunnel entrance.

Pieces of a 'Moll Bunker' shelter for the guard force can be seen on the side of the hill.

The 'Moll Bunker' located on the Bodnerbichl Hill would have looked like this one, near the site of Hitler's Tea House. The pieces that can be found on the Bodnerbichl Hill are the circular top, with iron ring for lifting this heavy piece during construction, a large piece of the side, and the doors. Most of these two-man guard force bunkers were simply blown in place at some point during the American occupation of the Obersalzberg.

In approximately 20 meters (65 feet) on this path you will come to concrete remains that are probably the foundation of a large air raid siren located on the Bodnerbichl hill (GPS N47.6320, E13.0417). Continue on this path down the hill. In about 30 meters (100 feet) you will pass a rectangular opening to a brick and concrete lined shaft, with six circular openings near the bottom. This was an access shaft to the network of conduits for electrical and communications cables that ran underground throughout the central Obersalzberg area, and several such shaft openings can be seen in this area.

Walk straight ahead to a flat rectangular concrete object – this was the cover of a large underground water cistern for supplying fire hydrants, principally for Hitler's Berghof. The elaborate Obersalzberg water system contained not only reservoirs and piping for water used in the homes and buildings, but also for an advanced fire fighting system, which even included sprinkler systems in some buildings. Turn right here and walk past the fallen trees (do not go downhill here, to the other path that you may see below). Continue past another cable shaft opening and walk downhill until you strike a rock path, then turn right on this path. Pass a square cable shaft opening and continue on this rock path around to the right.

In approximately 30 meters (100 feet) you will come to a large concrete artifact just to the left of the path. This was another water cistern or reservoir above the SS Barracks complex. The reservoir has two chambers inside it and water still flows through it.

The SS Kaserne barracks complex was located in the large open depression to your right front. The barracks were badly bombed in 1945 and the ruins were later demolished. In 2001 the building basements, an underground rifle range, and several tunnel corridors were excavated, leaving this pit-like depression. Continue past the reservoir until the rock path ends at a pile of rubble. This rubble consists of dressed stones and concrete from demolished Obersalzberg buildings, likely the Platterhof Garage (which was just above here), but possibly the SS Barracks buildings, demolished in 1952.

Retrace your path to the concrete reservoir. Just past the reservoir, turn right off the rock path and walk through the grass to the gravel path, and turn left. In approximately 50 meters (165 feet), just down the slope to the right is a huge bomb crater made by a large British bomb during the Royal Air Force attack on 25 April 1945, possibly a 12,000 pound 'Tallboy' bomb or 4,000 pound 'Cookie' bomb (several other smaller bomb craters are visible in this area). Just ahead along this path is a small concrete water reservoir for Hitler's Berghof house. The Berghof was originally just downhill directly in front of this position.

Continue past the water reservoir, noting the other bomb craters on the slope to your right. At least three bombs were direct hits on the Berghof during the 25 April 1945 Royal Air Force attack, and several other near misses caused severe damage. Turn left at the path intersection to walk past the Dokumentation Obersalzberg building (Guest House) and return to the parking lot. Note another cable shaft opening (which has been filled with gravel) just at this path intersection. As you walk toward the Dokumentation building, the Eagle's Nest can be seen on the mountain just in front of you. You will pass the glassed-over emergency exit to the Platterhof/Guesthouse tunnel system on the left, which is now the entrance to the bunker from the Dokumentation Obersalzberg display.

The air raid siren is the larger structure on top of the hill, just to the right of the trees, in this 1945 photo. The 'Moll Bunker' can be seen just down the hill to the right.

Shafts giving access to electrical and communications cables can be seen in several places on the Obersalzberg.

This water reservoir supplied the SS Barracks and other Obersalzberg buildings. The Obersalzberg water system was one of the most elaborate parts of the infrastructure, with several large reservoirs and miles of tunnels and piping for water supply and waste water removal. Much of this water system still flows water today, although some of it has fallen into ruin or been removed since 1945.

Seen from about your current viewpoint, the SS Kaserne had four main buildings: left – barracks building, right – gymnasium, center – mess hall and administration building, far right – garage and maintenance building.

The entry to the main SS barracks building featured a large sculpture of two men with swords and shields, and a plaque bearing the inscription SS KASERNE OBERSALZBERG. The sculpture was damaged during the April 1945 bombing attack.

Part of this SS Kaserne sculpture still exists today in a nearby town.

Hitler's Berghof was damaged by the bombing attack and fire set by the retreating SS soldiers. The huge bomb crater from a British 'Tallboy' or 'Cookie' bomb can be seen in the hillside just above the house.

Walking Tour No. 5

Hitler's Tea House and Moll Bunker Guard Shelter

NOTE: This walking tour involves somewhat strenuous hill climbing, especially on the way back. Good walking shoes and a walking stick are recommended. The total time for this walk is between two and two-and-a-half hours.

Begin at the Hotel zum Türken parking lot (Hintereck 2). Start down the road (in the direction of the Berghof site) and turn to the right onto the walking path into the woods, just across from the hotel (there is a blue pedestrian sign here – GPS N47.6340, E13.0435). A short distance inside the woods, off the path to the right, can be seen some stone foundations. These are the remains of the Unterwurflehen house, which was used during the Third Reich period by one of the SS administration officers.

Follow the gravel hiking path that slants down to the left. The emergency exit to Hitler's Berghof tunnel system that you saw in the tunnels beneath the Hotel zum Türken (Walking Tour No. 2) is in the valley to your left (it is difficult to reach, and is closed to the public).

The hiking path winds down the hill, curving around several water-filled depressions that are bomb craters from the April 1945 bomb attack. Continue on this walking trail through the woods, toward the right, and across the open area beneath the ski lift. The hillside beneath the ski lift, uphill from where you are standing, was once the site of an emergency exit to Bormann's tunnel system, but this exit has been buried. Follow the path downhill as it leads to a crossroads at the edge of the golf course, with a bench (GPS N47.6378, E13.0440).

Start downhill from this crossroads area, following the path sign to Unterau/Salzbergwerk (keep the golf course to your left), and in about 45 meters (150 feet), turn left on the small

This tunnel emergency exit led into the valley in front of the Berghof.

path that leads into the wooded area on the north side of the golf course, just past the first wooden trough for water run-off that crosses the main path (this side path is often muddy and the surrounding area is boggy – if you miss the turn onto this path you will start to go steeply downhill – turn around and look for the path turn-off shortly before the golf course (GPS N47.6382, E13.0442). Follow this path through the woods approximately 625 meters (2,000 feet) until it comes to a broad path leading to the right – this path leads to the site of Hitler's Tea House (do not go out onto the golf course itself).

At the end of the broad path is an overlook of the Berchtesgaden valley that was a favorite with Hitler and his closest associates, and this site appears very much now as it did in the 1930s. The wooden railing and bench are replacements, but in much the same style as the originals (the railing was rebuilt here for a 2004 German TV production called *Speer und Er* ('Speer and Him' – meaning Hitler). Hitler often paused here to gaze over into his native Austria to the north, or to converse with Eva Braun, Albert Speer, Sepp Dietrich, Heinrich Himmler, and others of his inner circle (GPS N47.6394, E13.0366).

As you turn around and look back from the overlook, Hitler's Tea House was built against the rock wall to your right front, just beneath the Mooslahnerkopf hill. Not to be confused with the Eagle's Nest (Kehlsteinhaus), which was not used as a tea house, the Teehaus on the Mooslahnerkopf was the building that Hitler visited almost daily while at the Berghof, where he enjoyed afternoon tea in a relaxed atmosphere with his inner circle. The Tea House survived the April 1945 bombing attack, but was torn down around 1952 with the other Hitler-related buildings in the area, and the ruins were removed in 2006 (a few foundation slabs remain).

Hitler's Tea House was a round pavilion with an attached kitchen. The overlook can be seen at the right.

Albert Speer regards a pensive Hitler at the Mooslahnerkopf overlook.

Please exercise caution when exploring this area – the Teehaus site is on the edge of a very steep slope.

Retrace your route to the path leading along the back side of the golf course, inside the woodline. As you walk back toward the path crossroads area, in about 300 meters (1,000 feet), you will see a path leading off to the left (north), at a small boulder (if you miss this turn, in a short distance on the left of the main path you will see a bomb crater depression with several old parts from a VW bus – turn around and look for the path turn-off at the small boulder). This path leads in a few meters to a stone foundation ruin. This was probably a forestry hut (not a Third Reich ruin), but just beyond this foundation on the slope below is an intact Moll Bunker guard shelter. This bunker was for the SS guards who walked the northern periphery of the Obersalzberg security zone, along a high chain-link fence that ran through this area. The fence posts were cut off after the war, but you can still see the bases of some of these posts and even part of the original fence material in the ground near this Moll Bunker.

It can be difficult to climb down from this point to visit this Moll Bunker, but if you return a short distance up the path and then go down into the valley to the left, you will reach a path that leads to the Moll Bunker. Notice how these bunkers were purely for shelter during a bomb attack, not for defense – it is difficult to even see out of the vision slits. Each of these Moll Bunkers originally had two wooden seats, as they were designed to shelter two guards (cramped quarters!), and some were linked by telephone systems.

Retrace your route to the start point.

Hitler enjoyed relaxing with Eva Braun and his closest associates at the Tea House.

Above: The Bavarian government demolished the ruins of the Tea House in 2006.

Left: One of the building's chimneys survived until the ruins were removed.

SS guards patrolled the security fence that ran around the Obersalzberg.

This bunker provided protection from bomb shrapnel for the SS guards along the northern edge of the Obersalzberg area. Some thirty of these two-man bunkers made by the Leonhard Moll company of Munich were emplaced at various locations around the Obersalzberg area and in the town of Berchtesgaden. Most of those located on the Obersalzberg were demolished with explosives after the Second World War, but at least two remain intact.

Youth Boarding House, Theater Hall, Antenberg Area

This tour takes about an hour. You can start from the Dokumentation Obersalzberg parking lot, or you can park a little closer to begin. Down the road from the parking lot, at the sharp curve to the right, on the left is an unpaved parking area, with a gravel road going up into the woods on the right. You can park here to start this tour (GPS N47.6301, E13.0388, Carl von Linde Weg). On the low hillside just above this parking area is a flat space – this is the site of a *Jugendpflegeheim*, or youth boarding house, that was built in 1939–1940. By this time there were no more youth groups visiting the Obersalzberg during war time, so the building was used by the local women workers in the home war industry. The wooden building was badly damaged in the 1945 bombing attack and the remains of the building were torn down around 1952.

Just down the main road from this parking area you can see broken rocks and concrete chunks beside the small stream just off the left edge of the road. These are the remains of the Antenberg Gate House, where SS guards controlled traffic driving to the Platterhof area from Berchtesgaden.

From the parking area, walk uphill a short distance on the gravel path, then turn right into the woods on a flat path (do not continue uphill on the rocky path). This path was once a paved road giving access to the Antenberg area, and you can still see curbs and some of the original roadway surface. The Antenberg was the site of barracks and other buildings for the Obersalzberg construction workers, as well as a large wooden theater hall built to entertain the workers. Anti-aircraft gun detachments were stationed here from 1943 to 1945. Just on the right at the start of the path, above the artificial pond, is a foundation of one of the Obersalzberg construction company administration buildings.

At the end of this path, as you reach a clearing that is often boggy and muddy, you can see a concrete ruin in the woodline in front of you – the remains of the Theater Hall (GPS N47.6290, E13.0354). This large wooden edifice was built in 1937 as an entertainment center for the workers on the Obersalzberg. Films and newsreels were shown several times weekly, and patriotic talks were given during the war, including speeches by Adolf Hitler. The collapsed ruin you see in front of you was the film projection room, made from bricks and concrete. Behind this part of the ruin can be seen the concrete foundation supports for the theater – this gives an idea of the size of this massive building. The roof of the theater collapsed from a heavy snowfall in March 1944 but was rebuilt. The theater survived the April 1945 bombing attack, but it was later torn down and the wood donated to rebuild the war-damaged Herz Jesu church in Munich. (The sign posted at the turnstile before the ruin warns that this is a farm area with the possibility of livestock present, and entry is at one's own risk.)

Ruins of several buildings of the Antenberg workers camp can be found in the woods below the open hillside that is just to the side of the Theater Hall ruins. If you wish to visit these building ruins, be advised that this farm area contains private property marked by fences, and you may encounter cattle or horses. Beneath this hill is an underground tunnel system built as an air raid shelter for the Antenberg workers (this tunnel is not accessible today). This shelter was never finished, but it provided protection for several hundred people during the 25 April 1945 bombing attack.

Retrace your route to the parking area.

The Obersalzberg Theater Hall provided films and other entertainment for the construction workers.

The Theater Hall appears at the upper right, with the camouflaged buildings of the Antenberg workers camp downhill to its left.

The Antenberg camp was bombed in 1945, but some of the building ruins remain today.

The unfinished Antenberg tunnel system provided shelter for the workers in the adjacent camp during the April 1945 bombing attack. When completed, the position seen here would have contained mounts for machine guns, similar to those seen in the Platterhof and Türken tunnel systems. Over 3,000 workers, military personnel, and their families took shelter in the Obersalzberg tunnel systems during the bombing attack. Only some five or six, who could not reach shelter in time, perished.

Klaushöhe and Buchenhöhe Settlements

This tour takes about an hour. Leave the Dokumentation Obersalzberg parking area (GPS N47.6307, E13.0415, Salzbergstrasse 45) and travel east on the road toward Oberau. After passing beneath the bridge that carries the Kehlsteinstrasse (Eagle's Nest Road) overhead, the top of the Coal Bunker (see Walking Tour 3) is just off the side of the road to the left (there is no place to pull over here, and the top of the Coal Bunker is unstable and very dangerous – keep off!).

Shortly beyond this on the right is a large parking area, with houses on the elevation behind. This is the Klaushöhe Settlement, which was built in 1939 as housing for families of Obersalzberg administration officers and married SS personnel (GPS N47.6310, E13.0527).

Turn uphill to the right at the end of the parking area, and follow the road as it curves to the left, following the signs toward Holzkäfer and Buchenhöhe. Travel 350 meters (0.2 mile) and park in a pull-off area on the left side of the road, just after you cross over the first bridge (GPS N47.6291, E13.0591). A large village of wooden barracks for construction workers was located up the hillside across the road from here, with other buildings located at this pull-off area.

Just downhill below this pull-off, to the left side (closest to the bridge you crossed), is a path leading to a type of air raid shelter called a *Splitterschutz* bunker – a concrete shelter built partly underground for protection from bomb shrapnel. Walk to the left downhill from the pull-off area, on a path that runs beside the deep valley on the right. You will come to a large metal eye sticking out of the ground – this was likely an anchor for a camouflage net. Angle left from here into the woods. You will pass a brick and concrete foundation on the left (one of the Obersalzberg construction workers buildings) with a shaft opening just beyond (watch out for this hole in the ground so you don't fall into it!).

The *Splitterschutz* bunker is located just past the shaft opening, to the right. Note how the entrances are located at right angles so that bomb blast or shrapnel could not go straight into the shelter (the entrances were originally closed by metal bunker doors). Other shelters like this were built at the upper end of the barracks area across the road, above Buchenhöhe, and also in Berchtesgaden itself.

Continue on this road. As you enter the Buchenhöhe settlement (GPS N47.6303, E13.0616, Buchenhöhe 1), most of the buildings on the main street in front of you are Third Reich period buildings, built from 1941 to 1944 as a model town for settlement of loyal Party members. Plans called for a store, restaurant, school, swimming pool, church, and even a cemetery for the self-contained apartment village, but most of these building plans were never realised. The Buchenhöhe settlement was not completed during the war, and the buildings were used to house refugee children from bombed German cities. The buildings on the lower (north) side of the settlement are part of a postwar Asthma Treatment Center.

(Note for the hungry – the Holzkäfer Restaurant, at the end of the main street in Buchenhöhe, is highly recommended – Buchenhöhe 40.)

Retrace your route toward the start point. Between Buchenhöhe and Klaushöhe you will cross three bridges, prime examples of the workmanship used in the Third Reich road building in this area. The middle bridge (GPS N47.6281, E13.0601) still has a stone on its concave side with the logo of Polensky and Zöllner, one of the construction companies, and the date 1941 (caution – this stone is difficult to see while driving – a safe viewing method is to walk to the bridge from a nearby parking area).

Obersalzberg administration personnel were provided housing at Klaushöhe.

Concrete bunkers covered with earth provided bomb shrapnel protection in the worker camps.

The largest Buchenhöhe building was the heating plant, which still showed camouflage paint in this postwar view.

The Polensky and Zöllner company (PZ) built many of the Obersalzberg area bridges.

Gutshof and Albert Speer's Studio

This tour takes about fifty minutes. From the Dokumentation Obersalzberg parking lot, take the road back toward Berchtesgaden. At the bottom of the first hill, where you turn left onto the main road back into Berchtesgaden, one of the primary SS guard houses was located on the other side of the road, to your right-front. The stone foundation remains, but please note that there is only a small pull-over area to stop here and view this ruin. The foundation can be best seen while driving on up the road that runs past the Hotel zum Türken (a right turn at this intersection).

Take the left turn toward Berchtesgaden. In 250 meters (0.3 mile), you will see a broad dirt road leading uphill to the left – this was the access road to the pig sty, horse stables, and hay barn that were part of the Gutshof complex. This model farm was built by Martin Bormann to indulge his hobbies of horse breeding and bee keeping, and expanded to include dairy cattle and pigs, but only parts of the business were ever profitable. (I do not advise you to try to park here and explore up this road; the hay barn took a direct bomb hit in April 1945 and its ruins were removed around 1952, and the ruins of the pig sty and stable building were removed sometime in the 1990s; there is really nothing to see up there now.)

Just past this dirt road, on the right, is the entry road to the Gutshof Golf Club (GPS N47.6332, E13.0329, Salzbergstrasse 33). Please note that from this side, you cannot turn directly into the drive – the turn is too tight – so turn into the bus stop just beyond the drive, then curve around and into the driveway leading down to the Gutshof buildings. (The road is narrow here – exercise caution.)

Bormann's Gutshof model farm now serves as a golf club and restaurant, and a ski center in the winter. These buildings housed the Gutshof employees and served as stables for the dairy cattle and other livestock, along with the apple cider presses and other farm machinery (the housing wing was torn down in 2007). The smaller building at the far end housed a waste water treatment plant. The decorative oval name plaque, bell, and large clock dial that you see near the golf club entrances at the front of the main building were originally mounted on the side wing that was torn down in 2007.

The Gutshof farm complex also included the greenhouse near Bormann's house, two large bee houses, and milk cooling houses located on the Antenberg and Scharitzkehl. An extensive tunnel system was begun here, that would have been large enough to provide underground vehicle access to the center of the Obersalzberg area (the tunnel entrances have been buried).

Across from the turn into the Gutshof drive is another driveway leading uphill to Albert Speer's house and architectural studio (GPS N47.6322, E13.0330, Antenbergweg 1). Speer was Hitler's favorite architect and so enjoyed his own house on the periphery of the Nazi elite area on the Obersalzberg. Both the Speer house (at the top of the road) and his architectural studio (to the left side of the driveway) are now private residences and the grounds are not open to the public – please observe the signs restricting trespassing.

Retrace your route to the start point, exercising care while entering the main road from these side driveways.

The primary SS gate house on the Obersalzberg was just below the Berghof.

The Gutshof farm had its own milk bottles for the milk produced by its herds.

Albert Speer designed his own architectural studio on the Obersalzberg.

Driving Tour No. 3

Hochlenzer, Alpine Road, Scharitzkehlalm, Göllhäusl

This tour takes about an hour. At the traffic circle near the Dokumentation Center, take the high road toward Hinterbrand. At 2.1 km (1.3 miles), turn right at the sign to Hochlenzer (GPS N47.6207, E13.0206, Scharitzkehlstrasse 6). Take the steep road downhill to the main buildings. You can park at the restaurant building, or in the parking area just downhill. Hochlenzer has been an Alpine guest house and restaurant for many years, and this was one of Hitler's favorite destinations for a walk, during his early years on the Obersalzberg – the restaurant displays some period postcards of Hitler visiting.

Children (and adults too!) may want to visit the *Sommerrodelbahn*, a metal bobsled-style track that's fun for all ages.

Return to the main road and continue to the south (turn right). In 800 meters (0.5 miles) you can park along the road to visit Graflhöhe, to enjoy one of their famous *Windbeutel* pastries ('Wind Bottle' – a puffed pastry).

Continue past Graflhöhe, and watch the right side of the road at 800 meters (0.5 miles). You can see the remains of the initial 1930s construction of the German Alpine Road – a curved overpass that was later bypassed when the road was reconstructed in the 1950s (if you wish to stop and visit there is a parking area across the road on the left, GPS N47.6066, E13.0248).

Continue and turn left at 500 meters (0.3 miles) onto the Scharitzkehl Strasse. Pull over at the stone building just on the left (GPS N47.6041, E13.0262). This building was a milk cooling house for the dairy herds of Bormann's Gutshof. Bormann appropriated the Scharitzkehlalm meadow as part of the Gutshof farm complex, and you can see how the waterway that runs through the meadow was lined with stone, as well as the stone bridge for the road, as part of

Hitler (left) visited the Hochlenzer guest house with his adjutant Wilhelm Brückner (right) and Reich Youth Leader Baldur von Schirach.

Bormann's construction projects. A tunnel running beneath the road was built in 1942 as part of the waterworks. The Scharitzkehlalm guest house at the end of the road is renowned for its good Bavarian food.

Return to the main road and turn left. Continue 2.5 km (1.6 miles) – drive through the parking area – the road appears to end here but it continues, and take the right turn following signs toward the Alpengastwirtschaft Vorderbrand. Turn to the right heading downhill, and pull over on the left when you reach the curve below the open hillside (if you reach the Alpengastwirtschaft Vorderbrand, you have gone too far). GPS N47.5937, E13.0181.

The small house back up on the hillside from which you came is the Göllhäusl. Early Nazi Party member and Hitler mentor Dietrich Eckart used this house as a hideaway from the Bavarian authorities in the early 1920s. Hitler was introduced to the Obersalzberg area when he visited Eckart at the Pension Moritz (which later became the Platterhof hotel), and Eckart later moved to the Göllhäusl to be even further away from public view. Eckart died in Berchtesgaden in 1923 and is buried in the *Altfriedhof* cemetery in town (see Berchtesgaden Walking Tour 2). After the Nazi takeover of the Obersalzberg area, this house was known as the Dietrich Eckart Hütte and was maintained as a shrine to Eckart. Hitler ordered that his sister Paula be evacuated from Austria in April 1945, and she was moved into the Göllhäusl when the U.S. Army occupied Berchtesgaden. The house was used by the American Forces Recreation Center as a youth retreat and was the last of the Nazi-era buildings to be relinquished by the U.S. Army (the house is not open to the general public).

From here you can retrace your route back uphill to the Obersalzberg area, or if you continue on this road past the Alpengastwirtschaft Vorderbrand it leads into Berchtesgaden (be advised this road is quite steep, narrow, and winding).

Adolf Hitler (right) hiked with Hermann Göring (left) and General Werner von Blomberg near the Göllhäusl. Hitler was an avid hiker in the Obersalzberg area in the early 1930s, before security concerns curtailed his public appearances, and he sometimes used these walks with other Nazi leaders to discuss policy decisions. Blomberg was Reichs minister of war and commander of the German armed forces, but he was dismissed from these posts in 1938 as part of Hitler's machinations to seize full control of the German military.

The former Dietrich Eckart Hütte still displays wood carvings from the Third Reich period.

Rossfeld Ring Road

This tour takes about ninety minutes. The Rossfeld Höhenringstrasse (High Ring Road), sometimes called the Rossfeld Panorama Strasse, was designed to complete the German Alpine Road on its eastern end. It is today a 15-km-long toll road (the toll varies per number of passengers, about 5.00–10.00 euro per vehicle) that offers spectacular mountain views in clear weather. (The road can also be driven in winter, except when closed by heavy snow – tire chains are required.)

The southern entrance and toll booth can be reached from the Klaushöhe Settlement (see Driving Tour 1), by turning off to the right from the road toward Buchenhöhe. From the Dokumentation Center parking area, take the road east toward Oberau for 1.1 km (0.7 mile) and turn right toward Klaushöhe and Buchenhöhe. Continue on this road 200 meters (650 feet) to the toll station to enter the Rossfeld Strasse (GPS N47.6303, E13.0536, Purtschellerstrasse 1).

Be advised that traveling the Rossfeld Ringstrasse involves a change in altitude of almost 600 meters (about 2000 feet) – this may affect children and others whose ears are sensitive to altitude changes.

The Rossfeld Strasse actually straddles the German-Austrian border, and was completed partly to provide access to heavy anti-aircraft (flak) batteries that were located on the high ground near the Rossfeld Ski Hut. After you leave the toll booth and make a left-hand curve, along this stretch of the road can be found remains of several concrete bunker and building structures in the woods on either side.

Optional – Pull over in the parking area on the right, 5.2 km (3.2 miles) from the toll booth (GPS N47.6227, E13.0747). Just up the hill across the road (follow the paths) are two sets of concrete foundation ruins (the second one is higher up the hill) that were probably associated either with the anti-aircraft batteries or cable car systems to bring supplies up to the gun batteries.

Continue up the road 7.7 km (4.8 miles) total from the toll booth to the Rossfeld parking area (GPS N47.6275, E13.0933). You can park and walk up to the high point above for a wonderful view of the Alps on both sides of the border. The view looking north toward the Untersberg Mountains will be familiar to fans of the movie *The Sound of Music*, as the final scene when the Von Trapp family crosses the mountains was filmed near here.

One of the flak battery positions was located just below this parking area – you can continue on the road for 200 meters (0.1 mile) and turn left into an unused parking lot – the flak guns were emplaced on this flat area. These Rossfeld flak guns were the famous '88' model. The Rossfeld Ski Hut, just down the road, was used as a headquarters for the flak batteries, and is today an excellent restaurant.

This concrete observation bunker guarded the Rossfeld Road.

These concrete remains were associated with the anti-aircraft guns emplaced along the Rossfeld Road.

The large caliber anti-aircraft guns emplaced on the Rossfeld had a wide field of fire.

Smaller flak guns, such as this 3.7cm model in a position near Oberau, were emplaced to deal with low-flying aircraft. Note the local boy examining one of the crew's helmets, which were kept close at hand on top of the gun revetment for instant use. In total there were eleven to fourteen flak battery positions with some 70 guns, ranging in size from 2.0cm to 10.5cm, emplaced around the Berchtesgaden area for protection of the Obersalzberg.

Flak (Anti-Aircraft) Batteries – Due to the need to protect Hitler's headquarters on the Obersalzberg, the Berchtesgaden area was ringed by some fourteen different flak positions, totaling thirty heavy guns (8.8cm and 10.5cm) and some forty light guns (2.0cm and 3.7cm). An underground command and control center was located in a tunnel system adjacent to Martin Bormann's air raid shelter. The flak guns were manned by a mixture of Waffen-SS, Luftwaffe, and Labor Service crewmen, and they engaged the British bombers on 25 April 1945, claiming to have shot down several aircraft.

You can turn around at the Rossfeld parking area or Ski Hut and head back the way you came, or you can continue and drive the entire Ringstrasse. This route passes through Oberau to return to the Obersalzberg via highway B319, which turns left (south) opposite the Auerwirt Guest House in Oberau (this building was remodeled in 1937 as a Hitler Youth Home and is today a restaurant – GPS N47.6518, E13.0590, Kirchplatz Au 2). Alternately, you can continue on into Unterau and drive into Berchtesgaden from the northeast on highway B305.

The Gasthaus Auerwirt was used as a Hitler Youth home during the 1930s.

CHAPTER 4

Eagle's Nest (Kehlsteinhaus)

Allow three hours for a thorough visit to the Kehlsteinhaus, although you can do this tour in two hours if you are pressed for time. The Kehlsteinhaus was the pinnacle of *Reichsleiter* Martin Bormann's building mania on the Obersalzberg, literally and figuratively. The project was an engineering marvel of its day – the house was built on a rocky spur of the Hoher Göll mountain, some 840 meters (2,756 feet) above the Obersalzberg, 1,834 meters (6,017 feet) above sea level. To reach this spur, a mountain road of some 6.5 km (four miles) was blasted into the rock, using only one hairpin curve (switchback), and five tunnels. The house itself is reached by a tunnel driven into the mountain, at the end of which is a large brass paneled elevator that rises into the building. The road and house were built in only thirteen months, to be presented to Adolf Hitler on his fiftieth birthday in April 1939 (although the house was finished before then, and most of Hitler's visits were in late 1938).

Even though the Kehlsteinhaus was a designated target for the April 1945 Royal Air Force bombing attack (the Allies thought there might be underground military facilities there, part of the mythical 'Alpine Redoubt'), it was not hit. Apparently it was too small a target and too difficult to pick out of the surrounding area from above. After the war the 'Eagle's Nest' became a popular stop for visiting American GIs, including such military celebrities as General Dwight Eisenhower (for a time, only officers were allowed to ride the elevator, and enlisted men had to use the footpath).

Due to intense lobbying by the Berchtesgaden district administrator, the Kehlsteinhaus was spared from the 1952 destruction of Nazi ruins and was returned to the State of Bavaria. It was opened to tourists as early as summer 1952 and is now operated as a restaurant by the Tourism Association, with portions of the proceeds going to a charitable trust. The house was restored and somewhat modernised, but its basic appearance today is much the same as during the Third Reich (the southern sun terrace was enclosed by glass, a large rear deck area was added, and there have been changes to the doors, windows, and lighting).

Who Named it the 'Eagle's Nest'?

By far the most common name for this building today is the 'Eagle's Nest', but the Germans never called it that, or 'Adlerhorst' or any other such name. The German name is 'Kehlsteinhaus', which means simply the House on the Kehlstein [Mountain]. The name 'Eagle's Nest' is often credited to French ambassador André François-Poncet, who called the site a *'nid d'aigle'* after a visit on 18 October 1938. However, British journalist G. Ward Price apparently coined the name 'Eagle's Nest' after his visit on 16 September 1938, a month before Poncet's visit. So Price should get credit for the name 'Eagle's Nest'. The building is often called 'Hitler's Tea House', but that is a misnomer as well. Although Martin Bormann was inspired to build the Kehlsteinhaus by Hitler's obvious fancy for the Teehaus on the Mooslahnerkopf, near his Berghof home, Hitler did not use the Kehlsteinhaus as an afternoon tea house, nor did he visit it often.

Despite its origins in the Third Reich, the Eagle's Nest is not treated as a history site today. There is one display of information panels in the sun terrace, covering the basic history of the site, but all the information is in German. There are no signs or markers in any of the rooms that explain their history during the Third Reich. Mainly, the Kehlsteinhaus is today simply a restaurant with fantastic views.

Only special tourist buses that are modified for the steep mountain roads are permitted to drive to the Eagle's Nest. Pedestrians are not allowed on the main road – you can hike up to the house and back down, but there are special paths for hikers. To tour the Eagle's Nest, buy a ticket for the bus at the ticket office that is located just below the main parking area on the Obersalzberg (signs point to Kehlsteinhaus / Eagle's Nest Bus – GPS N47.6312, E13.0424, Salzbergstrasse 45). You will want a roundtrip ticket (unless you plan to walk back down the hiking path), and your ticket will tell you which bus number and what time to board. The ticket price is discounted with a *Kurkarte* (hotel guest card).

I recommend going to the Kehlsteinhaus on one of the first buses in the morning. The Eagle's Nest is one of the most popular tourist destinations in Bavaria, with over 300,000 visitors during the five-month open period each year. The crowds can be extensive during the summer months, but they are usually smaller in the morning, and it is rewarding to be among the first people inside the building.

The first bus, which usually leaves around 7:30 each morning, lets you ride up with employees and early hikers. Check the schedule at the ticket window for the exact departure time. When this bus arrives at the parking area on the mountain, the interior of the house is not usually open to tourists yet, but you can spend thirty minutes or so exploring the outside while avoiding large tourist crowds, and then go inside. Taking this first bus up usually allows a quiet visit of an hour or perhaps ninety minutes before the main tourist buses start to arrive.

The weather at the Kehlsteinhaus is always a gamble. I've started up the mountain when it was perfectly clear – not a cloud in the sky – but when I arrived about twenty minutes later, it was cloudy or foggy … you just never know. In fact, although the Kehlsteinhaus is officially scheduled to be open from mid-May until mid-October, the opening is often delayed by the need to repair winter damage to the road, and snowfalls later in May can close the house for a few days. Early October snowfalls can cause an earlier than anticipated closure for the winter. The safest bet is to plan your visit during June to September. Also, it can be chilly up there – you are almost 1,000 meters (3,250 feet) higher in elevation than where you boarded the bus, and the temperature can drop surprisingly. Please note also that the difference in elevation can affect sensitive ears, such as young children's. And keep in mind, while you take this remarkable bus ride up the steep and curving mountain road – there has never been an accident with one of these Kehlsteinhaus public buses.

Whichever bus you take, as soon as you get off the bus at the upper parking area, you have to proceed to a ticket window in the building to the side to get your return time stamped on your ticket. Most people spend at least an hour at the Eagle's Nest, perhaps ninety minutes if you want to eat at the restaurant. You may want to allow more time during peak tourist hours when the house will be crowded, or if you want to explore extensively outside. Please allow about fifteen minutes before your departure time, to ride the elevator back down and get in line for a return bus. So if you plan to eat at the Kehlsteinhaus restaurant and see the main sites, it is usually a safe bet to schedule your return for two hours after your arrival. If you find that you wish to return at a different time than what is stamped on your ticket, this is normally not a problem, unless the buses are all crowded. Ask the bus driver or ask at the ticket window.

After you get your return time stamped on your ticket, proceed to the tunnel entrance, noting the large plaque that says ERBAUT 1938 (Built 1938) above the entrance. This was the only structure here until the 1950s; the other buildings were added for the tourism business. The tunnel is closed by two sets of huge bronze doors. The outer set originally had handles designed in the shape of lions, but these were taken as souvenirs by American soldiers in 1945. If you look closely at the doors you may see names and dates that the visiting Allied soldiers scratched into their surfaces in 1945.

Proceed down the 126-meter-long tunnel (413 feet). The light fixtures are the originals, but the tunnel was not damp and cold during the Third Reich period, as it is today. When visitors were present, warm air flowed out of vents along the lower walls. As you walk, imagine having to drive one of the Mercedes limousines used by the Nazi elite down this tunnel … and then having to drive it back out in reverse!

Before you enter the domed waiting room for the elevator, take a close look at the wall at the end of the tunnel. During construction in 1938, the workers used dark colored stones to form a swastika in the wall. These stones are still there, but their color has been disguised to make it difficult to pick out the swastika shape now. In the elevator waiting area please stand to the right side, so as not to block the exit route for those who will get off the elevator. There is a sign posted for No Photography … please do not take flash photographs, as the shiny brass interior of the elevator reflects photo flashes into others' eyes, and you don't want to bombard those who are exiting the elevator with a series of annoying flashes as if they were at a press conference.

Hint – Get on the elevator last, so you can get off first, and proceed straight to the main room, which was the focal point of the building.

The elevator car had leather benches where the Nazi elite could relax during their ride, but these have been removed for more standing room. The telephone and clock on the wall by the operator are original, and there is a lighted indicator on the wall showing the height as you ascend 124 meters (407 feet) to the house. Originally there was a second car below the main car, which guards and support staff used to ride up to the house, exiting in the basement. This lower car was removed during renovations after the war.

Soldiers of the 101st Airborne Division open the doors of the Eagle's Nest tunnel for military visitors in May 1945.

The original tunnel door handles were bronze lions.

The author's father (right) visited the Eagle's Nest in early 1946.

American soldiers drove their jeeps into the Eagle's Nest tunnel.

The elevator opens at the top into a side hallway that contains restrooms and coat racks. To visit the inside of the house, turn right out of the elevator and go through the doorway straight ahead, into the main dining room of the Third Reich period. Turn right and proceed through the next doorway and down the steps into the main hall.

This hall featured prominently in photographs of Adolf Hitler and his guests during the Third Reich period and also in snapshots taken by U.S. Army personnel in 1945. The walls appear to be solid stone, but the house was actually constructed of a concrete base with granite blocks applied on the outside and sandstone on the inner walls of the main hall. Hitler actually visited the Eagle's Nest on only a few occasions (probably fewer than twenty), as he supposedly did not like the pressure changes from the rapid rise in elevation or the possibility of lightning striking the elevator machinery. Hitler's main visits were to show the new structure off to visiting dignitaries in 1938 and 1939, and he never used the building as a tea house. Martin Bormann and Eva Braun did far more entertaining in the Kehlsteinhaus. One of the most lavish occasions in this room was the celebration following the wedding of Eva's sister Gretl to SS General Hermann Fegelein in June 1944, when a day and night of dancing and dining took place here.

Originally this room held a small round table surrounded by comfortable chairs on a lush carpet, another smaller rectangular table with chairs, other stuffed chairs scattered around the room, and an expensive Gobelin tapestry over the fireplace for decoration.

The fireplace shows the completion date of 1938 flanked by male and female figures on horseback on the rear panel, and the red marble surround and mantel (a gift from Italian leader Benito Mussolini) show chips and missing pieces from the initial souvenir hunting in the summer of 1945. This taking of fireplace pieces by Allied soldiers became so bad that eventually large signs were posted warning visitors that any soldier caught looting would be tried by court-martial. If you look closely you can see names and dates scratched into the marble by visiting American soldiers and Germans. The large windows were originally made to be lowered into the wall for an open air view of the mountains, but these windows were replaced in the 1950s and the present windows do not lower. (Some guides will tell you that the Kehlsteinhaus building appears today just as it did in 1945, but these windows are only one of many changes to the house since then, including some significant structural changes.)

There is a souvenir stand in the corner of the hall beside the fireplace, that sells books in English. They also sell DVDs and video tapes, but American visitors must make sure to buy these in the NTSC format (not PAL), for viewing in America.

Go through the smaller doorway next to the entry doorway and down a short flight of steps (the wooden door is a post-war addition). This room is called the Scharitzkehl Room because it overlooks the Scharitzkehlalm meadow far below. This room is sometimes erroneously called the 'Eva Braun Room' today, but there is no period reference to support the idea that this was a special room for Eva Braun. The walls are paneled with decorative cembra pine (Swiss pine), but most of the panels are replacements for those looted in 1945 (as are some of the light fixtures, both here and in the main hall). The original windows in the Scharitzkehl Room could be lowered into the casings, but these 1950s replacements do not lower.

A doorway with its original bronze doors leads onto the Sun Terrace. Originally, this was open air – the glass was added in 1957. The information panels along the wall explain the history of the Kehlsteinhaus.

Proceed through the Sun Terrace to the open terrace at the back of the house. This terrace

The original dining room had only one long table for guests.

The main hall had chairs and tables comfortably arranged at the marble fireplace.

Hitler visited the Eagle's Nest with Martin Bormann's wife Gerda (left), Joseph Goebbels' wife Magda, and Eva Braun.

A large dining table was installed in the main hall for the wedding celebration of General Fegelein and Gretl Braun in June 1944.

In August 1945 U.S. General Mark Clark (right) showed famous signatures on the Eagle's Nest table to his counterparts from France, Great Britain, and the Soviet Union, General Antoine Béthouart, General Sir Richard McCreery, and General Alexei Zheltov.

The red marble fireplace was defaced by Allied soldiers in 1945.

The Scharitzkehl Room was a comfortable salon paneled in rustic pine.

Adolf Hitler enjoyed a moment of solitude on the Kehlsteinhaus sun terrace. This photo may have been taken during one of Hitler's few private visits to the Kehlsteinhaus. Most of his trips up the mountain were during diplomatic visits by national leaders and ambassadors, when Hitler enjoyed 'showing off' his new dramatic construction. The open air arches in the sun terrace had glass windows added in 1957.

is much larger than it was during the Third Reich period; in fact, the original terrace ended in a low stone wall just past this doorway, where several photos show Hitler's visitors along with Eva Braun and her sister Gretl posing for the camera. This wall was removed and the large seating area added in back and around to the side in the 1950s to accommodate restaurant visitors.

You can walk from here up the steps toward the *Gipfelkreuz* (summit cross) for a breathtaking view of the surrounding mountains in nice weather. Along the way you will notice some concrete artifacts off the right side of the path (exercise care to view these – they are close to the edge of the mountain), as well as other concrete and iron artifacts protruding from the rocks along the pathway. These remains may be associated with the 3.7cm anti-aircraft guns that were mounted behind the Kehlsteinhaus, or with a cable car system that brought supplies up during construction of the building.

Optional – Experienced hikers may want to follow this trail past the summit cross, through the rocks and down, to reach the remains of a wall that formed a base for the SS guard fence running behind the Kehlsteinhaus (GPS N47.6080, E13.0499). This trail takes about thirty minutes to reach the wall and involves some steep areas. There are hand railings and rock and wooden steps, although these can be slippery, and good hiking boots are recommended.

Return to the back of the building. The entry doorway near the Kehlsteinhaus plaque leads into the kitchen area, a former guard room, and an office that was provided for Hitler, although he did not use it (not open to the public). Continue around to the right (the north side of the house). This side of the building exhibits some of the more obvious structural changes since 1945. The only original doorway here is the arched doorway – the flattop doorway was converted from a window around 2004. Additionally, windows have been added in the part of the building housing the elevator machinery (the part with the tall antenna on the roof).

From here you can walk down beside the house on a path that leads eventually to the bus parking area (about fifteen minutes), or you can return to the elevator waiting area through one of the doorways here. Please stand to the right as you wait for the elevator, so as not to block the exit for those arriving. (Restrooms are in the hallway here, opposite the elevator.)

I suggest that you plan to take the return elevator to the bus parking area at least fifteen minutes prior to the return time stamped on your ticket, to view some interesting items in the parking area. If you did not get a chance before you rode the elevator up to examine the bronze tunnel doors for 1945-period soldier graffiti, you can do so now. As you continue out of the tunnel entrance, turn to the left and walk past the building with the ticket window and snack/souvenir stand. Just at the other side of this building you can see a small arched doorway closed by a bronze door. This leads to a service tunnel running beside the main tunnel to the elevator shaft, and housing machinery including an original U-Boat engine as an auxiliary power generator (this tunnel and the U-Boat engine are off-limits to the public).

If you back up slightly (watch for bus traffic) and look up over the roofline above the tunnel door, you can see what appears to be a vertical stack of rough stones beside the trees. This was clever camouflage to cover the exhaust pipe of the U-Boat engine, part of the general design of the Kehlstein road and structures to blend in with nature as much as possible.

During the bus ride back down, count the tunnels as you pass through them. The second

The wall at the rear of the sun terrace where Eva Braun posed at the Kehlsteinhaus was removed after 1950. In contrast to Hitler's few visits, Eva Braun and her family and friends were frequent visitors to the Kehlsteinhaus. Martin Bormann also did considerable entertaining there, often ordering the house to be opened late at night or snow to be removed from the road in the middle of the winter.

This concrete relic behind the Eagle's Nest may be associated with the anti-aircraft guns that were emplaced on the ridge behind the house.

A high metal guard fence ran around the Kehlstein area and was mounted in places on long rock walls.

When it was built and when these American soldiers visited in 1945, the Eagle's Nest had no large rear terrace.

The north side of the house had only one door when these GIs visited in 1945, and camouflage netting still hung from the roof.

The Schwalbennest (Swallows Nest) Tunnel on the Eagle's Nest road had remains of camouflage netting in 1945.

Only one hairpin curve was used in the building of the Kehlstein Road, at the Scharitzkehl curve.

Nearby is a tunnel in the rock face whose original purpose is unclear, but which may have been meant as an air raid shelter or a test boring for the final tunnel to the elevator.

The Zigeuner (Gypsy) Tunnel is called the Gamstunnel (Chamois Tunnel) today.

The Schwalbennest (Swallow's Nest) Tunnel is a rather simple construction, with stone cladding on only one side.

The Südwest (Southwest) or Hochlenzer Tunnel (sometimes called the Recktunnel today) has elaborately finished stone entrances.

This side tunnel in the Südwand (South Wall) Tunnel may have been built as an air raid shelter.

and fifth tunnels (the longer tunnels) both have side chambers about in the middle, possibly meant as protection against air attacks along the road. If you watch closely, you may be able to catch of glimpse of these arched openings on the left sides by watching the reflection of the bus headlights on the tunnel walls.

CHAPTER 5

Königssee Area Sites

The Königssee, or Royal Lake, is a long narrow Alpine lake surrounded by towering mountain sides and cliff faces, located just south of Berchtesgaden. The lake is a favorite with tourists today, and a tour of the lake can reveal several sites associated with the Third Reich. Due to the summer tourist crowds, it is best to arrive early and take one of the earlier boats. This guide to the Third Reich sites requires the complete (longer) boat tour, so plan on at least three hours and thirty minutes for the trip, not counting time spent waiting in line for the boats or time spent sightseeing or dining at St. Bartholomä (the first stop). Königssee boat tour schedules and fees can be found at the Tourist Information Center (*Kurdirektion*) in Berchtesgaden, or on the internet at www.seenschifffahrt.de/en/koenigssee/.

To reach the Königssee boat dock area, leave Berchtesgaden on highway B20 to the south – take the exit from the traffic circle in front of the train station that is marked Königssee, driving beside the Tourist Information Center (*Kurdirektion*). Travel 4.2 km (2.6 miles) to the Königssee parking area (GPS N47.5929, E12.9872, Seestrasse 3). Enter the parking area just past the region's only McDonald's restaurant. The entire Königssee parking area is a fee lot – you must buy a *Parkschein* (parking ticket) at any of the machines in the lot (see Appendix B). Buy the day ticket – the other parking tickets available will not give you enough time for this tour (there is a discount by using your *Kurkarte* Tourist Card). After you park, walk out of the parking area and turn left onto the main street that goes through the village of Königssee, which consists primarily of tourist shops and restaurants.

Tickets for the boat rides are sold at the ticket building at the lake edge past the Hotel Schiffmeister (turn right when you get to the monument to Prince Regent Luitpold). This hotel was one of the buildings used by the Obersalzberg staff and German military leaders in their final retreat before advancing Allied forces in May 1945. For a tour of Third Reich sites associated with the Königssee, you will want to buy a round-trip boat ticket to Salet. Different routes are offered – you may buy a ticket that goes straight to Salet, or your ticket may give you a stop at St. Bartholomä. Whichever route you take, your ultimate destination is the Obersee, at the Salet stop. When you purchase your ticket, take note of the times for the final return boats from both Salet and St. Bartholomä, as there is no way back if you miss the last boat. In tourist season, the lines that form for the last boats can be quite long, so I recommend leaving earlier. It's a good idea to pick up a tour pamphlet in English at the ticket window, as the narration during the boat ride is in German (usually with a Bavarian accent).

The Hotel Schiffmeister at the Königssee lake was used to house high ranking visitors to the Berchtesgaden area.

Your ticket will tell you which pier to stand on to wait for your boat. If possible, choose a seat that will give you a view out the right side (starboard) of the boat, for both the outgoing and return trips. You will pass the small Christlieger island on the left, and the narrator will tell you about a small red cross on the cliff wall to the right, which is a memorial to a boat accident in 1688 in which seventy religious pilgrims drowned. As the lake opens up to the left is the famous 'Malerwinkel', or Painters Corner, where countless renderings of the most famous view of the lake have been made. You can see this view for yourself, looking down the lake toward the white and red domes of the St Bartholomä chapel, with the Watzmann mountain on the right and peaks of the Steinernes Meer range straight ahead. You may be able to pick out the Eagle's Nest (Kehlsteinhaus) on the peak behind the bay to the left (if you can't see it from your side of the boat, you can look on the return trip).

Just past the Malerwinkel on the left is a waterfall called the Königsbachfall. As the fall runs down the cliff face it has scoured out several tanks that form natural pools, and these were a favorite recreation area for Eva Braun and her family and friends. At the base of the fall is a small beach where Eva was filmed and photographed doing gymnastic exercises (you can see this better from the right side of the boat on the return trip.)

The cliff face on the right side, opposite the base of the Königsbach waterfall, was the site of a planned tunnel system that would have served as a headquarters for Hitler and the main staff of the military high command, if they had retreated to the 'Alpine Fortress' for their last stand. This large tunnel system was never actually begun, although test borings were made in the rock face, close to the water.

One of the most famous scenic views in the area is looking down the lake from the 'Malerwinkel'.

Eva Braun enjoyed visiting the Königssee to practice gymnastics and bathe in the Königsbach waterfall.

Above left: Adolf Hitler visited the Königssee and St. Bartholomä.

Above right: Hitler posed for his photographer Heinrich Hoffmann at the Obersee lake.

On a subsequent visit, Hitler moved a few meters to the right and sat on a boulder at the lake edge.

In a short distance the boat will stop for a while and the narrator will play a trumpet or flugelhorn to demonstrate the 'Echowand'. You will probably hear one or two echoes of the brass horn, but in earlier days the boatmen shot off black powder pistols which gave seven echoes.

Your boat will likely stop at the St. Bartholomä landing. If time permits you may wish to stop here to enjoy the beautiful scenery or perhaps a meal in the well-known restaurant beside the chapel (a former hunting lodge for the Bavarian kings). Or you can reboard the boat to continue to the Salet landing and the Obersee.

Get off the boat at the Salet landing and walk on the footpath past the restaurant building and into the woods. A walk of about ten to fifteen minutes will bring you to the Obersee lake, which was once part of the Königssee but was cut off by a landslide. The beautiful Obersee, surrounded by mountains, was visited by Adolf Hitler on at least two occasions.

As you reach the Obersee lake you will see a fishing hut at the shore. A short distance to the right of this hut is a pair of large boulders at the water's edge, where Hitler posed for photographs. The water level varies with the season and rain/snowfall; you may find these rocks only partly submerged, as they were when Hitler visited, or they may be surrounded by shallow water.

Hermann Göring had a hunting lodge in the mountains above the Obersee. Göring was an avid hunter and outdoorsman with hunting lodges at several locations in the Reich. He decorated his houses and lodges in a rustic style with hunting trophies and carved wooden furniture. Despite his bulk, Göring even climbed Berchtesgaden's Watzmann mountain (with assistance).

Return on the path to the Salet boat landing. Standing at the pier, or looking back just after the boat leaves, you may be able to catch a glimpse of a distinctive notch in the mountains beyond the Obersee. Below this notch (but not visible from the lake) is the site of a grand hunting cabin built for Hermann Göring, who was an avid hunter and outdoorsman. Only foundation ruins remain of this cabin, which can only be reached by a strenuous hike through the mountains.

Take the boat from the Salet landing back to St. Bartholomä if you wish, or straight back to the main Königssee dock (about one hour by boat). If you get a seat on the right side on the return trip, you can get a better view of the Königsbach waterfall and the beach area where Eva Braun and her friends visited, and the Eagle's Nest on the mountain behind the Malerwinkel.

The view at the Königssee docks is still very similar to that seen by visitors during the Third Reich period.

APPENDIX A

Miscellaneous Area Sites

Other Third Reich associated sites can be found in the Berchtesgaden area but are not covered in the tours in this book. A good reference to these sites is the 'Third Reich in Ruins' webpage, www.thirdreichruins.com/bgaden.htm.

Two sites of particular interest can be found in Bad Reichenhall, 19 km (12 miles) from Berchtesgaden. The former Mountain Artillery Troops Barracks (now called Hochstaufen Kaserne) is located in the Karlstein area of the city (GPS N47.7240, E12.8642, Nonner Strasse 23). The barracks are not open to the public, but are worth a drive by to view the Third Reich period decorations on the gate building.

A relic from the Third Reich that was originally located on the Obersalzberg can be seen in Bad Reichenhall today. An inner courtyard of the Platterhof hotel had a large fountain featuring a figure of Atlas, a work by the famous Third Reich sculptor Josef Thorak. This 'Atlas Fountain' was moved to Bad Reichenhall in the 1950s, and it can be seen today in the spa district. The fountain is located in the *Kurgarten* park, in front of the *Gradierwerk* (GPS N47.7279, E12.8808). The *Gradierwerk* itself is an interesting site. This building allows salt water to trickle over bundles of sticks, and inhaling the moist salt-laden air is recommended for lung health.

The Berchtesgaden area also has several family-friendly tourist sites. The most famous of these (and one of the biggest tourist attractions in the area) is the *Salzbergwerk*, or salt mine. This mine gave Berchtesgaden its prosperity for many years and is still in operation. Today visitors can take a tour through unused parts of the mine. The main parking area is on the west side of B305, across the river from the salt mine itself (GPS N47.6393, E13.0138, Salzburger Strasse 24). Tourists are treated to a trip through the mine on a small train, including a change of levels by sliding down a wooden rail, as the miners used to do. The tour includes a boat trip across a salt water lake, and views of translucent salt crystals in various hues of brown and pink. Salt crystals made into lamps and other souvenirs can be purchased at the shop.

The *Sommerrodelbahn* is a metal bobsled style track, on which one rides a small car down the hill ... it is like an amusement park ride, except that the rider controls the brake and the speed. The ride is located near the Hochlenzer restaurant (GPS N47.6204, E13.0185, Scharitzkehlstrasse 6), www.hochlenzer.de/rodelbahn.html.

A favorite with children is the *Murmeltiergehege*, an open-air animal and bird sanctuary on the Obersalzberg. The entrance is near the Göring Adjutancy building, and the displays

A large stone eagle and military wall paintings can still be seen at the barracks in Bad Reichenhall.

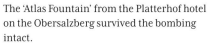

The 'Atlas Fountain' from the Platterhof hotel on the Obersalzberg survived the bombing intact.

The Atlas Fountain can now be seen in Bad Reichenhall.

include birds of prey and Alpine marmots (*Murmeltiere*). Park at GPS N47.6325, E13.0469, Hintereck 9, and follow the *Adler und Murmeltiergehege* signs.

Other area sites with interest for a family visit include the *Kugelmühle* mill for grinding stone spheres with water power (www.gasthaus-kugelmuehle.de/geschichte_engl. php), the Berchtesgaden Heimatmuseum (local history museum, www.heimatmuseum-berchtesgaden.de), Maria Gern church (www.stiftskirche-berchtesgaden.de/maria-gern. php), and the Jenner cable car at Königssee (www.jennerbahn.de/de/englisch).

Webpages for Museums and Businesses
Berchtesgaden tourism webpage – www.berchtesgadener-land.com/en/home
Eagle's Nest (Kehlsteinhaus) – www.kehlsteinhaus.de/en
Dokumentation Obersalzberg – www.obersalzberg.de
Königssee boat schedules, ticket prices – www.seenschifffahrt.de/en/koenigssee

The Third Reich period eagle and soldier murals still appear at the entrance to the Bad Reichenhall military barracks.

APPENDIX B

Hints for Visitors

The best times to visit Berchtesgaden and the Obersalzberg are late May / early June or late September / early October. The heavy summer tourist crowds are smaller during these periods, but the Eagle's Nest is open (subject to unusual weather conditions).

The Berchtesgaden Tourist Information Center (*Kurdirektion*), across the river (traffic circle) from the train station, has a wealth of useful information on area sights, guided tours, local schedules, hiking paths, museums, hotels, restaurants, etc. If you arrive without hotel reservations, they can help you find a place to stay. I recommend you pick up a good Berchtesgaden area map from the helpful staff at the main desk inside.

Your hotel should issue you a *Kurkarte* tourist card for each visitor (you are charged a daily fee for this, in addition to the room price). The *Kurkarte* can be used for discounts at many area museums, attractions, and restaurants (always ask if they give a tourist discount), and free local bus transportation. The *Kurkarte* can also be used for a discount at some parking ticket machines. (The *Kurkarte* is sometimes called a *Gästekarte*, or Guest Card.)

Hints for Parking

Most of the parking lots along the streets in Berchtesgaden are pay lots, requiring you to buy a parking ticket for a certain length of time. These parking tickets, called *Parkscheine*, are available from ticket machines at the sides or ends of the lot (look for the sign that says *Parkscheinautomat*). To use the machine, first look to see if it has a slot to take a *Kurkarte* or *Gästekarte* – this will give you a discount. There will probably be a button on the machine with a British flag – this will give you instructions in English on the screen. Insert either your *Kurkarte* or the necessary amount of euro coins for the length of time you want to park, then press the green OK button. The small ticket will be dispensed. You must place this ticket on your left side dashboard so that the expiration time can be seen through the windshield.

Note that the main parking lot on the Obersalzberg, for the Dokumentation Obersalzberg display and the Eagle's Nest bus ticket office, requires a *Parkschein* at most times (sometimes parking is free, and is so-noted on the *Parkschein* machines). Many of the public parking lots in Berchtesgaden that require a *Parkschein* may have marked reserved spaces, so not every space may be allowed for parking with a *Parkschein*.

It can be difficult to find a parking space along the main streets in Berchtesgaden, but if you don't mind a little uphill walking, you can park in the lot beside the Esso fuel station

Look for this sign to buy a ticket at a pay parking lot.

The parking ticket machines may give a discount if you use your *Kurkarte* (Guest Card).

on Bahnhofstrasse (entrance at GPS N47.6305, E13.0040, street address Bahnhofstrasse 21). Buy your *Parkschein* at the machine near the entrance and post it in your vehicle, then walk to the back of the lot, opposite the Esso station. You will find a sidewalk that passes between some houses and then goes up a flight of steps to the left. When you come out at the street (you are on Bahnhofstrasse, just up from the Esso station), turn right and stay on this sidewalk as it curves up the hill, and you will reach downtown Berchtesgaden after a short walk.

You may find some short-term parking spaces that require a *Parkscheibe* parking disc. These are usually provided by the rental car company, or you can buy one at any fuel station or auto parts store. Parking spaces requiring a *Parkscheibe* will be marked with a sign that shows the maximum parking time. Set the rotating disc on your *Parkscheibe* to your arrival time, rounding up to the nearest half-hour, and place it inside the left corner of your windshield or dashboard. (This disc must be blue in Germany – the red disc sometimes used in Austria is not valid in Germany.)

If you choose to park in an underground parking lot in Berchtesgaden, please bear in mind that these lots are often small with narrow parking spaces and low ceilings. Vehicles larger than a small minivan should definitely avoid these lots. You get a parking ticket as you drive in (you may have to push a button on the machine to get the ticket). Carry this parking ticket with you, because you will pay at a machine at the pedestrian entrance to the lot, before you return to your vehicle, not as you drive out. The ticket machines (usually labeled *Kasse*) normally have a button you can push to get English on the screen. They will accept euro bills and coins and possibly credit cards. Stick your ticket into the slot, matching the arrows, pay the fee on the screen, then your change and ticket will be returned to you. You normally have ten minutes in which to leave after you pay. Stick the paid ticket into the small machine at the exit (*Ausfahrt*), and the gate will rise. Note that there are some reserved spaces in most underground lots, for specific vehicles (these spaces will often have a sign like a license plate), or for women (*Frauen Parkplatz*).

Other Useful Information

A cell/mobile phone is almost a necessity for touring Germany today. If your personal cell phone will not work in Germany (check with your provider before your trip), you can buy a prepaid (no contract) cell phone in Germany. Most larger airports and train stations have a Mobile Center or store that sells cell phones, which are called a 'Handy' in Germany. You can buy an inexpensive basic phone and then load it up with the desired amount (you buy a certain amount of euros, not minutes – most people will find 20–25 euros sufficient for basic in-country use during a two-week trip). You will probably also want to buy a battery charger for your phone.

If you plan to buy any DVD films or VHS tapes at the Eagle's Nest or other souvenir or book shops, be aware that these will normally not play in America. Europe uses the PAL standard, while the U.S.A. uses the NTSC standard, and they are not compatible. To play European DVD/VHS on an American TV, you must have a multi-system player and television. Check while you are shopping – some DVDs and tapes are available for Region 1, or region-free, for viewing in the U.S.A.

Most German street signs insert a hyphen between the names on the sign, thus – Koch-Sternfeld-Strasse – but I have omitted these hyphens in the tour directions in this book.

Parking spaces marked with this sign require a *Parkscheibe* during the noted hours, for the maximum time shown.

After setting the dial to your arrival time, place the *Parkscheibe* on your dashboard.

Public toilets can be found in the following locations (look for signs to Öffentliches WC, or just WC, or 00 (an old German sign for toilets): Berchtesgaden – Tourist Information Center (*Kurdirektion*), Bahnhof (train station), Schießstättbrücke guard house, below the parking lot on Ludwig-Ganghofer Strasse, Bergfriedhof cemetery

Obersalzberg area – Dokumentation Obersalzberg museum, Berggasthof restaurant, Eagle's Nest, Königssee – Tourist Information Center at the main parking lot

APPENDIX C

Glossary of German Words and Phrases

Ausgang/Ausfahrt – exit

Bahnhof – train station

Betreten auf eigene Gefahr – Enter at your own risk

Betreten Verboten – No Trespassing

Eltern haften für ihre Kinder – Parents are responsible for their children

Flak – anti-aircraft guns (abbreviation of *Flugabwehrkanone* or *Fliegerabwehrkanone*)

Forellenzucht – trout farm

Friedhof – cemetery

Gauleiter – Nazi regional leader

Gipfel – mountain summit

Kaserne – barracks, military post

Kein Eingang – No Entry

Kein Durchgang – No Pass-Through

Kriegerdenkmal – war memorial

Kurdirektion – tourist information center

Kurkarte (Gästekarte) – tourist pass, discount card

Luftwaffe – German air force

Marktplatz – main square in a city or town

Parkscheibe – parking disc for time-limited parking places

Parkschein – paid ticket for parking lots

Reichsleiter – Nazi Party high political leader

SA – Sturm Abteilung – Hitler's 'Brown Shirts' storm troopers

SS – Schutzstaffel – elite Nazi guard force, including Hitler's bodyguards

Stollen – tunnel

Stube – parlor, pub

Trachten – old style native costume, can include Dirndl dresses and Lederhosen pants

Wehrmacht – German armed forces

W.C. – public toilets (water closet)

Zentrum – center of town

Photo Credits

U. S. National Archives, Record Group 111SC, U.S. Army Signal Corps Collection – 17, 18, 23, 26 (bottom), 28 (top), 47 (bottom), 48 (top), 69, 86 (top), 88 (top), 124 (top), 129 (top), 133 (bottom), 134 (top left)

U.S. National Archives, Record Group 242, Heinrich Hoffmann and Eva Braun Photo and Film Collections – 38, 44 (bottom), 46 (top), 59, 77 (bottom), 80, 81 (top), 82 (bottom), 87 (bottom), 102, 103, 105 (top), 110 (top), 127 (top), 128, 130 (bottom), 132 (top), 139 (bottom)

U.S. National Archives, Record Group 342FH, Records of U.S. Air Force Commands – 28 (bottom), 44 (top left), 97 (top), 100

U.S. National Archives, Record Group 373.3, Records of the Defense Intelligence Agency – 58 (bottom), 73 (bottom), 107 (bottom)

Author's collection – 12, 13, 19, 20, 30 (bottom), 31 (top), 33, 34 (center, bottom), 37, 43 (bottom), 44 (top right), 46 (bottom right), 48 (bottom), 49, 51 (top right), 53, 54, 58 (top), 60 (top left), 62 (top, bottom right), 65, 67, 70 (bottom), 71 (bottom right), 73 (top), 79, 82 (top), 83 (top), 88 (bottom), 89 (top), 92, 93, 94, 95, 97 (bottom), 98 (top), 99 (bottom), 101, 104 (bottom), 105 (bottom), 108, 110 (bottom), 111 (bottom), 113 (bottom), 116 (bottom), 118, 119 (bottom), 120, 124 (bottom), 125, 129 (bottom), 132 (bottom), 133 (top), 134 (bottom), 135, 136, 139 (top), 142, 144 (center, bottom), 145, 147, 149

Period postcards (author's collection) – 4, 14, 21 (bottom), 26 (top), 27, 31 (bottom), 47 (top), 50 (bottom), 57, 62 (bottom left), 70 (top), 71 (top), 74, 75, 76, 77 (top), 78, 84 (bottom), 87 (top), 89 (bottom), 91 (bottom), 98 (bottom), 99 (top), 107 (top), 111 (top), 127 (bottom), 130 (top), 138, 140 (top right), 144 (top)

Courtesy Airborne Yellow Archives – 34 (top)

Courtesy David Dionne – 24

Courtesy Nancy Tarsitano Drake – 90

Courtesy Ray and Gilda Northcott – 134 (top right)

Courtesy Ingrid Scharfenberg – 21 (top), 39 (top), 56, 68, 71 (bottom left), 84 (top)

J.I.O.A., *German Underground Installations* (1945) – 60 (bottom), 64

Adolf Hitler: Bilder aus dem Leben des Führers (1936) – 116 (top)

Der Freiwillige (1975) – 119 (top)

Deutschland erwacht: Werden, Kampf un Sieg der NSDAP (1933) – 35

Hoffmann, *Hitler abseits vom Alltag* (1937) – 83 (bottom)

Hoffmann, *Hitler in seinen Bergen* (1938) – 41 (bottom), 91 (top), 115, 140 (top left, bottom)

Ich Kämpfe (1943) – 81 (bottom)

Moderne Bauformen (1937) – 32

Schönleben, *Fritz Todt* (1943) – 41 (top)

Schuster-Winkelhof, *Adolf Hitlers Wahlheimat* (1933) – 46 (bottom left), 51 (top left)

The Epic of the 101st Airborne (1945) – 39 (bottom)

Troost, *Das Bauen im neuen Reich* (1943) – 30 (top), 114

Wikipedia, Bundesarchiv Collection – 52, 113 (top)

Yank, the Army Weekly (1945) – 60 (top right)

Ziemke and Helm, *Moritz Mayer* (1930) – 50 (top)

Selected Bibliography

12th Armored Division Association, *The Hellcats* (Paducah: Turner Publishing, 1987).

Adolf Hitler: Bilder aus dem Leben des Führers (Hamburg-Altona: Cigaretten-Bilderdienst, 1936).

Adolf Hitlers Wahlheimat: Zweiundzwanzig Zeichnungen von Karl Schuster-Winkelhof, Begleitworte von Walter Schmidkunz (Munich: Münchner Buchverlag, 1933).

Beierl, Florian M., 'Dokumentation und Destruktion', *Obersalzberg Journal* 1 (2009), 1–13.

Beierl, Florian M., *History of the Eagle's Nest* (Berchtesgaden: Verlag Plenk, 1998).

Beierl, Florian M., *Hitlers Berg: Licht ins Dunkel der Geschichte* (Berchtesgaden: Verlag Beierl, 2004).

Beierl, Florian M., *Projekt Kehlstein* (Berchtesgaden: Verlag Beierl, 1993).

Below, Nicolaus von, *At Hitler's Side* (London: Lionel Leventhal Limited, 2001).

Berchtesgaden: A Brief Story of Its Past and Traditions (Berchtesgaden: Berchtesgaden Recreation Area, n.d. (*c.* 1950).

Berchtesgadener Land, Deutschland-Bildheft Nr. 139 (Berlin: Universum-Verlagsanstalt, n.d. (*c.* 1936).

Berchtesgadner Land (Garmisch-Partenkirchen: Verlag Hans Huber, n.d. (published under U.S. occupation, *c.* 1946).

'Bilder die noch keiner sah: Mit Hitler bis zum Ende', *Quick* 17 (1964), 36.

'Blowup at Berchtesgaden', *Life* 32 (1952), 41–42.

Büchner, Bruno, *Gebirgskurhaus Pension Moritz* (Obersalzberg: priv. publ., 1928).

Campbell, Christy, 'Bavaria Cashed in on Hitler's House', *The Telegraph* 961 (1998), http://www.portal.telegraph.co.uk/htmlContent.jhtml?html=/archive/1998/01/11/whit11.html (accessed 29 November 2004).

Chaussy, Ulrich and Christoph Püschner, *Nachbar Hitler: Führerkult und Heimatzerstörung am Obersalzberg* (Berlin: Ch. Links Verlag, 2001).

Cowan, Howard, 'Man Who Built It Casts Doubt on Nazi Redoubt', *Chicago Daily Tribune*, 15 May 1945.

Davidson, Max, 'A World of Evil and Hope Amid the Dark Pine Trees', *The Observer* (2005), http://www.guardian.co.uk/travel/2005/mar/13/germany.observerescapesection (accessed 21 April 2005).

Dietrich, Otto, *The Hitler I Knew* (New York: Skyhorse Publishing, 2010).

Effern, Hainer and Klaus Ott, 'Die Bank und ihr Hotel', *Süddeutsche Zeitung* (2010), http://www.sueddeutsche.de/bayern/obersalzberg-die-bank-und-ihr-hotel-1.366746 (accessed 18 October 2010).

Effern, Hainer and Mike Szymanski, '17 Millionen für Ausbau des NS-Dokuzentrums', *Süddeutsche Zeitung* (2013), http://www.sueddeutsche.de/bayern/obersalzberg-millionen-fuer-ausbau-des-ns-dokumentationszentrums-1.1693366 (accessed 12 June 2013).

'Es muß ein Stück vom Hitler sein', *Stern* 13 (1960), 14–17.

'Eva Braun's Album', *Life* 23 (1947), 48–54.

'Eva's Private Poses', *Life* 22 (1947), 37.

Exner, Gunther, *Hitlers zweite Reichskanzlei* (Cologne: Verlag Wissenschaft und Politik, 1999).

Fabritius, Silvia, *Adolf Hitler und Eva Braun auf dem Obersalzberg* (Obersalzberg: Verlag Silvia Fabritius, n.d [1984]).

Fabritius, Silvia, *Obersalzberg: Before and After the Destruction* (Berchtesgaden: Verlag Silvia Fabritius, n.d.[1985]).

Flinn, John, 'Rising Above the Past', *San Francisco Chronicle* (2006), http://www.sfgate.com/travel/article/RISING-ABOVE-THE-PAST-Cherished-by-Hitler-2515110.php (accessed 15 August 2006).

Frank, Bernhard, *Der Obersalzberg im Mittelpunkt der Weltgeschehens* (Berchtesgaden: Verlag Plenk, 1995).

Frank, Bernhard, *Hitler, Göring, and the Obersalzberg* (Berchtesgaden: Anton Plenk KG, 1989).

Frank, Bernhard, *Secret Kehlstein* (Berchtesgaden: Verlag Plenk, n.d. [1995]).

Frankel, Andrew, *The Eagle's Nest* (Berchtesgaden: Verlag Plenk, 1985).

Führer durch das Berchtesgadener Land (Berchtesgaden: L. Vonderthann & Sohn, 1936).

Galante, Pierre and Eugène Silianoff, *Voices from the Bunker* (New York: Doubleday, 1990).

Geiss, Josef, *Obersalzberg: Die Geschichte eines Berges Von Judith Platter bis Heute* (Berchtesgaden: Verlag Josef Geiss, 1952).

Geiss, Josef, *Obersalzberg: History of a Mountain from Judith Platter Until Today* (Berchtesgaden: Verlag Josef Geiss, 1980).

Hamm, Florentine, *Obersalzberg: Wanderungen zwischen Gestern und Heute* (Munich: Zentralverlag der NSDAP, 1941).

Hanisch, Prof. Dr. Ernst, *Der Obersalzberg, das Kehlsteinhaus, und Adolf Hitler* (Berchtesgaden: Verlag Plenk, 2000).

Harper, David, *Your Complete Guide to Berchtesgaden* (Berchtesgaden: D. Harper, 1997, and Verlag Plenk, 2005). (This book is by far the best guide in English to all the sights in the area. It is literally full of history and practical information. Check at the Berchtesgaden Tourism Center (*Kurdirektion*).

Hartmann, Max, *Die Verwandlung eines Berges unter Martin Bormann* (Berchtesgaden: Verlag Plenk, 1993).

Hitlers Berghof, 1928-1945: Zeitgeschichte in Farbe (Kiel: Arndt-Verlag, 2000).

'Hitlers Erbe', *Der Spiegel* 27 (1964), 40–43.

Hitler, Adolf, *Hitler's Secret Conversations* (New York: Farrar, Straus and Young, 1953).

Hoffmann, Heinrich, *Hitler abseits vom Alltag* (Berlin: Zeitgeschichte Verlag, 1937).

Hoffmann, Heinrich, *Hitler in seinen Bergen* (Berlin: Zeitgeschichte Verlag, 1935).

Hoffmann, Heinrich, *Hitler Was My Friend* (London: Burke, 1955).

Hoffmann, Heinrich, *Hitler, wie ihn keiner kennt* (Berlin: Zeitgeschichte Verlag, 1932).

Holzhaider, Hans, 'Ein Geheimnis wird gemacht', *Süddeutsche Zeitung* (2010), http://www.sueddeutsche.de/bayern/bunkeranlagen-am-obersalzberg-ein-geheimnis-wird-gemacht-1.60758 (accessed 1 May 2012).

Holzhaider, Hans, 'Nachbar Bormann', *Süddeutsche Zeitung* (2005), http://www.sueddeutsche.de/reise/obersalzberg-nachbar-bormann-1.879802 (accessed 25 November 2011).

Holzhaider, Hans, 'Spurensuche am Täterort', *Süddeutsche Zeitung* (2011), http://www.sueddeutsche.de/bayern/obersalzberg-spurensuche-am-taeterort-1.1074152 (accessed 12 June 2013).

'Houses that Adolf Built', *Parade* 2 (1939), 51–55.

Hudson, Alexandra, 'Luxury Hotel Opens at Hitler's Alpine Retreat' (2005), http://www.reuters.com/newsArticle.jhtml?type=ourWorldNews&storyID=7772106 (accessed 4 Mar 2005).

'InterContinental Hotel At Hitler Site Sparks Row' (2005), http://www.hospitalitynet.org/news/154000320/4022308.html (accessed 9 March 2005).

Irving, Clive, 'A Hotel Too Far?', *Condé Nast Traveler* (2005), http://www.cntraveler.com/features/2005/11/A-Hotel-Too-Far (accessed 3 January 2013).

Junge, Traudl, *Until the Final Hour* (New York: Arcade Publishing, 2004).

Kinzer, Stephen, 'Berchtesgaden Journal; An Unspoiled Alpine View, a Legacy of Demons', *New York Times* (1995), http://www.nytimes.com/1995/09/13/world/berchtesgaden-journal-an-unspoiled-alpine-view-a-legacy-of-demons.html (accessed 21 April 2005).

Korman, Seymour, 'GIs Celebrate with Hitler's Own Champagne', *Chicago Daily Tribune*, 7 May 1945.

Krause, Karl Wilhelm, *Kammerdiener bei Hitler* (Bochum: ZeitReisen-Verlag, 2011).

Lang, Jochen von, *The Secretary* (New York: Random House, 1979).

Leidig, Michael, 'Outrage at Third Reich Museum' (1999), http://www.zundelsite.org/english/zgrams/zg1999/zg9911/991120.html (accessed 19 January 2005).

Linge, Heinz, *With Hitler to the End* (New York: Skyhorse Publishing, 2009).

Lochner, Louis, 'Hitler Builds Secret Hideaway on Mountain Peak', *Reading Eagle* 51 (1939), 2.

Maierbrugger, Arno, '"Hotel Hitler" Concept Proves a Failure' (2010), http://gulfnews.com/business/tourism/hotel-hitler-concept-proves-a-failure-1.687990 (accessed 3 January 2013).

McGovern, James, *Martin Bormann* (New York: William Morrow & Company, Inc., 1968).

Miller, Marjorie, 'Nazi Symbol to Return to German Hands', *Los Angeles Times* (1995).

Mitchell, Arthur H., *Hitler's Mountain* (Jefferson, North Carolina: McFarland & Company, Inc., 2007).

Moor, Paul, 'The Old Order: Berchtesgaden Seven Years After', *Harper's Magazine* 205 (1952), 57–67.

'Mrs. Adolf Hitler', *Life* 18 (1945), 34.

Nerdinger, Winfried (ed.), *Bauen im Nationalsozialismus: Bayern 1933–1945* (Munich: Klinkhardt & Biermann, 1993).

Neul, Josef, *Adolf Hitler und der Obersalzberg* (Rosenheim: Deutsche Verlagsgesellschaft, 1997).

Neumann, Conny, 'The Führer's Flagstones', *Spiegel* (2010), http://www.spiegel.de/international/germany/the-fuehrer-s-flagstones-the-twisted-legacy-of-hitler-s-mountain-retreat-a-686221.html (accessed 3 April 2010).

Obersalzberg Bilddokumentation (Berchtesgaden: Verlag Plenk, 1976).

Offizieller Ausstellungskatalog, 2. Deutsche Architektur- und Kunsthandwerkausstellung (Munich: Verlag Knorr & Hirth K.G., 1939).

Osborne, Jim R., 'Return to the Berghof', *After the Battle*, 60 (1988), 50–53.

Paterson, Tony, 'Furor in the Eagle's Nest', *World Press Review* (1995), http://www.findarticles.com/p/articles/mi_m1453/is_n6_v42/ai_16878719 (accessed 21 April 2005).

Penrose, Anthony (ed.), *Lee Miller's War* (Boston: Little, Brown and Company, 1992).

Peterson, Michael Ray, *Ames to Berchtesgaden* (n.p., 2008).

Phayre, Ignatius [William George Fitzgerald], 'Hitler's Mountain Home', *Homes & Gardens* (1938), 193–195.

Pratt, Lt. Col. Sherman W., U.S. Army (Ret), *Autobahn to Berchtesgaden* (Baltimore: Gateway Press, 1992).

Ramsey, Winston G., 'Obersalzberg', *After the Battle* 9 (1975), 1–35.

Rapport, Leonard and Arthur Northwood, Jr., *Rendezvous with Destiny: A History of the 101st Airborne Division* (Washington: Infantry Journal Press, 1948).

Rhomberg-Schuster, Maria, *Historische Blitzlichter vom Obersalzberg* (Salzburg: Selbstverlag der Verfasserin, n.d. [1957]).

'Royal Air Force Bomber Command Campaign Diary, April and May 1945', http://www.raf.mod. uk/bombercommand/apr45.html (accessed 26 December 2012).

Ryback, Timothy W., 'The Hitler Shrine', *The Atlantic* (April 2005), 131–134.

Ryback, Timothy W., and Florian M. Beierl, 'A Damnation of Memory', *The New York Times*, 12 February 2010.

Schaffing, Ferdinand, *Der Obersalzberg: Brennpunkt der Zeitgeschichte* (Munich: Albert Langen / Georg Müller Verlag, 1985).

Scharfenberg, Ingrid H., *Das historische Haus 'zum Türken' und seine Bunkeranlagen am Obersalzberg* (Berchtesgaden: priv. publ., n.d. [2010]).

Scharfenberg, Ingrid H., *Die Bunkeranlagen am Obersalzberg* (Obersalzberg: Verlag Ingrid Scharfenberg, n.d.).

Scharfenberg, Ingrid H., *History of the Hotel Türken* (Berchtesgaden: priv. publ., n.d. [2002]).

Schmid, Matthias, 'Wenn die Steine reden …', *Berchtesgadener Heimatkalender* (2011), 65–77.

Schöner, Hellmut (ed.), *Das Berchtesgadener Land im Wandel der Zeit* (Berchtesgaden: Verein für Heimatkunde des Berchtesgadener Landes, 1982).

Schöner, Hellmut, Ilse Lackerbauer and Fritz Hofmann, *Die verhinderte Alpenfestung* (Berchtesgaden: Verlag Anton Plenk, 1996).

Schöner, Hellmut and Rosl Irlinger, *Der alte Obersalzberg bis 1937* (Berchtesgaden: Berchtesgadener Anzeiger, 1989).

Schroeder, Christa, *Er war mein Chef* (Munich: F.A. Herbig Verlagsbuchhandlung, 1985).

Schwaiger. Rosemarie, '„Hotel Hitler": Millionenflop in Berchtesgarden' (2010), http:// diepresse.com/home/wirtschaft/international/597256/index.do?from=suche.intern.portal (accessed 3 January 2013).

Seerwald, Michael E., *Hitlers Teehaus am Kehlstein* (Berchtesgaden: Verlag Beierl, 2007).

Seidler, Franz W., *Phantom Alpenfestung? Die geheime Baupläne der Organisation Todt* (Berchtesgaden: Verlag Plenk, 2000).

Sions, Sgt. Harry, 'The House That Hitler Built', *Yank, the Army Weekly*, 4 (1945), 1–5.

Speer, Albert, *Inside the Third Reich* (New York: Macmillan, 1970).

Taggart, Donald G. (ed.), *History of the Third Infantry Division in World War II* (Washington: Infantry Journal Press, 1947).

The Epic of the 101st Airborne (Auxerre (France): 101st Airborne Division Public Relations Office, 1945).

The Obersalzberg and the 3. Reich (Berchtesgaden: Verlag Plenk, 1984).

Tuohy, William, 'Berchtesgaden: Beauty and an Ugly Past', *Chicago Sun-Times* (20 Sept. 1987), http://business.highbeam.com/392330/article-1P2-3846096/berchtesgaden-beauty-and-ugly-past (accessed 12 May 2013).

Turner, John F. and Robert Jackson, *Destination Berchtesgaden* (New York: Charles Scribner's Sons, 1975).

Valenti, Isadore, *Combat Medic* (Tarentum, PA: Word Association Publishers, 1998).

Warner, Gary A., 'German Resort Wants Visitors to Look Beyond Former Resident', *Stars and Stripes* (21 September 2006), 26–28.

Webster, David, *Parachute Infantry* (Baton Rouge: Louisiana State University Press, 1994).

White, Nathan, *From Fedala to Berchtesgaden* (Brockton, MA: Keystone Print, 1947).

Will, Rosemarie and Liane Gruber, '60 Jahre Insula', *Berchtesgadener Heimatkalender* (2011), 134–142.

Wortsman, Peter, 'Who Let the Dogs Out?', http://www.citizenculture.com:80/inside/original/who_let_the_dogs_out.htm (accessed 10 April 2007).

Ziemke, Magdelene and A. Helm, *Moritz Mayer* (Berchtesgaden: A. Helm, 1930).

Manuscript and Audiovisual Sources and Interviews

After Action Report, 101st Airborne Division G-3, 4 May 1945, Record Group 407, Box 14362, U.S. National Archives, Washington, DC.

Beierl, Florian M., 'An Interview with Professor Edward T. Linenthal about Historical Relics and Monumental Protection of Sites around Hitler's Berghof on the Obersalzberg near Berchtesgaden, Bavaria', Online Publication of the Obersalzberg Institute e.V., Berchtesgaden, 2010, http://www.obersalzberg.org/media/publikationen/Linenthal.pdf.

Beierl, Florian, Interviews with author, Obersalzberg, June 2001, May 2005.

Eva Braun's Photo Albums, Record Group 242-EB, and Eva Braun's Motion Pictures, Record Group 111-ADC-1183, U.S. National Archives, College Park, Maryland (Archives II).

Finken, Raimund, Interview with author, Obersalzberg, June 2001.

G-3 Journal, 3rd Infantry Division, 4–6 May 1945, Record Group 407, Box 6228, U.S. National Archives, Washington, DC.

Heinrich Hoffmann Photograph Collection, Record Group 242-H, U.S. National Archives, College Park, Maryland (Archives II).

Interview of Paula Hitler by U.S. Army, 5 June 1946, Records of the Army Staff (G2), Record Group 119, U.S. National Archives, College Park, Maryland (Archives II).

Joint Intelligence Objectives Agency (J.I.O.A), *German Underground Installations, Part Three of Three*, J.I.O.A. Final Report No. 3, Germany, September 1945.

Maps and Plans, Berchtesgaden and Obersalzberg Buildings, Collection Baupläne Berchtesgaden 1933–1945, Bavarian State Archives, Munich.

Scharfenberg, Ingrid, Interviews with author, Hotel zum Türken, Obersalzberg, 1999–2001, 2003–2006, 2007, 2009, 2011–2013.

U.S. Army Military History Institute, Senior Officers Oral History Program, Project 1974 – LTG John A. Heintges (Vol. II).

War Department Collection of Captured German Records, Record Groups 260-NS, 260-NSA, and 242-HPKTC, U.S. National Archives, College Park, Maryland (Archives II).

Index